Zoo Chow

Zoo Chow

Jim Thurber

Selected Poems: 1964–2016

Zoo Chow

Published by Cassidy Bayou Books
552 La Guardia Place #9
New York, NY 10012

First Printing 2018
Book design & layout by Florri DeCell
Book production by Lisa Rappoport
Cover illustration by Oriana Lewton-Leopold

ISBN 978-0-9889694-1-4

for Detta

Jim Thurber's work has been published in many
magazines, journals, and anthologies, including:

Stafford's Road
Hollow Orange
Synapse
Illuminations
Peace & Gladness
Calapooya Collage
Suisun Valley Review
NIE Journal
Thyme and the River
Or
Cow
Berkeley Daze
The Pentameron
Manifesto of Red & Blue
East Bay Review
Mountains in Flight

Many of his poems have also previously appeared in *cardboard boxes*

Poetry is the art of being kidnapped by circumstances.
—A. Codrescu

So much for poetry, the Jezebel that kept me treacherous
company all these years.
—Roberto Bolaño

Contents

Early Poems

from The Book of Dead Bathtubs

(for Luis Garcia)

not rapid or bleedy   enough
nothing bulletin from nothing   not fast enough
        flower dawn night high steep red Kid
double give   junk moon   certain black pie
      razor, rolls-royce
            rolling highfreak super skin   179
fluid looey   powerful eye-hair grope
      needle stop stop skid offf

ii

san francisco   space freakeye terror night boogie   pink   shit
      flesh
            sewer liquors   gasoline high kundalini crush
fuzz   brainbird egg cracked soft yellow brain suck lunar blowjob
      brain job.

            gentle suicide of an orange, orange girl orange hair
                        orange pubic
stop 10 stop 20 stop stop

iii

        this little gem
    is still alive   the wheat
    is dry-brown   the dust
          rises and comes back
        far from home

    precious gem

It's a Trip

It's a trip
we go on
a trip we take
for the sake of
movies wrenched

with desire
we trip
out to take
it back out
to wrench it
back into
a trip we go on
a trip we take

That's On

that's on
the end of
the hook,
bait dropped
into the mouth
on the end of
underneath
taking it from
the bait
by the mouth
that's on the hook on
the end

There Is No More

there is no more
giving
in when there is
no more sin.

This is not a
sin so give
in, give
in.

if this is
a sin then
you cant give
in you cant win

What Do I Expect

what do I expect
my fellow men
to give me for this:

a kiss, the lips
of the siren
down the street
apart from
where you are

saw you
go out.

The Clear Expression

the clear ex-
pression the clear
expression of it
the clear impression
of it the clear
impression of it

the clear expression
the clear impression

of it

SEGAKI

self of whose a ghost?
    in the anguished aftermath
  salt & fine blood of the spoken —

IS THIS
      wrapped in my loneliness underwear
   I whistle around myself
     waiting for the indian
    coming along the trail

  with thirteen legs

1964-65

Lecture on Modern Poetry

trying to make a cantaloupe
out of words
he makes a big cantaloupe.
Western poetry is full of
such distinctions.
To cut it in half
his knife must have been
very sharp.
When I saw him
he was holding,
bewildered, the two
halves one in each
hand. "I never conceived
of them being separate,"
he said, turning
to place one half
            in the refrigerator.
            Having emptied
            something from the
            scale of justice
            his hands had assumed
            he ate the other half
            slowly.
            Feast of solitary beauty.
            In the morning, unseen,
            turning on the refrigerator
            shelf, the other half
            of the conception
            had disappeared. Basho
            would have called a painter
            saying, "Paint this half of
            the moon orange
            & sprinkle its guts
            with pale-lemon seeds."

2

he says "smooth"
when he hears
the word's sound
is like the
cantaloupe looks
after it has been
sliced.
he would say
the same thing
about the way
an apple looks
after the knife
has its exercise
& even about
the soft white pine
left open-eyed
by the fast metal
of the axe.

Tips from the Telephone Book:

'if you burn the inside of the oven with an exploded potato or
something, soak a cloth in ammonia and let it stay on the burned
places an hour or so, after which you can scrape the spots clean
without harming the enamel'

while reading this the potato
in the oven
began to explode. I
turned off the heat
opened the door, salted
my fingers and discovered
there is not much you can do
to make a potato taste differently
without harming the enamel.
(this does not imply

that you are to pour
the ammonia on the
potato.)

2

Yarn Preserver:

'Discourage moths attacking yarn you are storing away
by winding it around a mothball.'

Thinking to Write

Thinking to write
whatever exists
to be
written
dissolves
in the thought
of it.

Forms of Flying

when so unspeakably bound to it
we understand   the MYSTERIES   (MISTRESS
The perfumed one the one who dances   (O, not those peacock
wings again!
        When so unspeakably (bound & gagged, eek!

THAT WE NOW TRY TO RECALL
Oh, a cult of recaller s?

        THE WORLD OF

THE POEM

        ARISETH & FLOURISHETH

NOW & FOREVER MORE   {
                  {   eternal
         bliss

         } eternal bliss
         }

& DAUNSINGE!

Peyote the Kid

for Chick Reeder

PAGES OF THE BOOK
BEGINNING: 'When doomsday turned her head...'

we were all caught looking:

THE CITY IS PASTED TO A SPLENDID EYE SUSPENDED
    IN THIS WHIRLPOOL
              OF ENERGY
watching itself walk up & down
drive cars back
and forth   THE CITY

IS A BREATH OF THE BREATHING THAT ENERGY

"ONE IS IMPOSSIBLE"

★

the horizon
has mountainous fingers
behind which are the mountainous mountains

of the palms of my hands? (can't make it out

★

10

& some large frescoes painted on the sky
detailing History
The babe at the center is called
Beauty because she solved the problem
of "Texture"
saying "Life is the only Texture — don't you think?"

I remember the texture of Winesap apples
tasted on frosty days in the orchard
sugar filling them full of sweetness
but her skin, the sweetness of it
      not in words
the texture of it

Peyote the Kid part II

HAVING ACCOMPLISHED THE FIRST 35 MISSIONS

      we can now get back to contemplating

        the cold potato

        ★

      cold potatoes
   so sweet and looking
       so old:
next to the cold
     apple I'm eating:

    you're nothing!

        ★

SECOND LESSON —
     second by second,

       eat the cold apple.

Live as though you were going out of existence

Did you say you might?

Jewels pasted up in the Void?

Whose poems did you say?

★

Eating cold apple: discover exact texture —
        1st)   no heartbeat;   ODE to apple:
        Ripening green crescent
        teardrop in my palm
        green cold tea in mouth
        twilight in stomach.

WHO'S EATING THIS APPLE ANYWAY?

        : you little jewel

★

Imagine, he said to me, going swimming without

        the possibility of drowning

★

FORGET THE SECRET?
Not only did I forget the secret in my pocket
        sitting down on it
        and breaking it but
        then decided
        it was useless
        anyway.

★

Back to the THIRD LESSON:

> The black cat who looks as though he
> has been rolled
>   in dust (and fights with his brother
> Bach of Bach's Pussycats Inc)
>   are just so much frosting
> on the grass

>   eating from their rice bowls
>   the way they do
>   hunched & black
>   tonguing trout out
>   of the stream
>   of all things

*

FOURTH LESSON: LOVE,
        love, love me do

>   Because it is a great love affair & she
>   actually has a job all these alarm clocks
>   are set up like mine fields & she
>   reads The House on the Borderland
>   every night

>   because noted the words
>   'authentic gooseflesh'

TONIGHT HE WILL MATCH HIS FLESH AGAINST ANY
    GOOSE GOING!

*

I put out the light and strike sparks
        through her fur.

          Silver shad scales so iridescent
 skin   white wave-wake of back
          speckled with light, writing
a poem to it as I lie beside it,
         around it, over it
underneath me a divine sleeky beast
         frozen blond waterfall of hair
over my white rock body

★

I come to sleep
And wake inside her sleep.
The cat gnaws in its fur,
The wind slides around the eaves,
The ghosts walk and as lovers
We turn with time, suspended
In our void where hours come to rest.
I come to sleep
And wake inside her sleep.
It is a warm wind
A wind of jade and eyes.

Dream

I could see that they knew what they were doing
the story which is impossible to unravel
to get straight two brothers   blond,
or me a fugitive
blocked by somebody in the alley—
no witnesses of myself being murdered
by someone who looked kind of like me
which is implausible
in the underworld of dream events
to which poetry puts its name

the top of the pen drooped off when I wanted to
go out on the roof

they beat the two blond brothers to death one of which
is me or I know him—I look on in utter shock
& he looks back in utter shock we're shocked

BY DROWNING STRAPPED TO BOARDS FORCING
OUR HEADS UNDER EACH TIME THE VIOLENT LOOK
OF COLORS FORCED TO ETHEREAL

nothing we said nothing no
no lips no moans beseeching dirges praises
        what could we say o please don't?

I could see that they knew what they were doing

Cities

Shut Off Again

Coming home to our suburban house
RED notice on the doorknob
like a flag. Our lights and gas were cordially
turned off by your friendly utilities pals after you
ignored their various, sundry & repetitive warnings.

"I was just on my way down to pay the bill."

"We're real sorry, hate to do it but we're just doing our job."
They drive off down the hill in their white truck
with the black letters on the sides.

Red-tagged a decade ago my memory flips back to '67.
The City was cracking down hard on squatters.
We held out 'bout four months on McAllister St.
Weather beaten gray faux Victorian, tenants evicted,
landlord disappeared. Our luck — electricity
was overlooked; doors not boarded up yet.

I call an old friend to reminisce —
'Member that, man? No fucking gas? Used a Coleman.
"Things are OK as long as the toilet flushes."

Rent strikes to break the slumlord's backs.
"Almost a dozen men & women, 2 adolescents &
two little babies, we toughed it out through the winter.
Bob Gordon lived downstairs & directed the strike.
We had one of us to haul the garbage; tied in with the Diggers
for food — got their cart to come by every so often.

Burned out cars & a whole garage filled
with rotting garbage.

"When they turn off the water &
you ain't got a place to shit
is generally when I moved on."
We formed a bucket brigade when that happened.

Crossed over the neighbor's lawn and tapped his hose.
A five gallon can hauled the most, took strong arms.

Bill & Aaron brought in the dope.
A warm bathroom to lock yr self in, roomy —
safe place to fix, no paranoia
I traced the shower drops on the wall,
seeing diamonds.

Bob Gordon went to New York to drive taxi.
Ron left his old lady & Diane left her old man,
made a baby together & split to Massachusetts.
Paula & her two brilliant boys raised on acid,
moved out & took up with Bob Stubbs.
Rick & Polly hung on for quite a while.

Tom Sheil drifted in and out like the beaded
& feathered Zen Indian he'd become, always
smiling and playing the flute. Wally, shaved head, bare-footed,
wore mechanic coveralls, went naked indoors,
his own mind in itself able to destroy households & commune
            peace at will.
He ate all our food & smoked all the dope, played piano & guitar
at the same time, foot & toes holding guitar on floor to strum & pluck.
His gift to charm, give massages, his silences soothed us.
He covered walls with schizophrenic paintings; Blake's ". . . marks
of weakness, marks of woe" in every face he painted.
Jessie, a Bob Dylan look-alike save red hair, came by
every so often without his three girls and guitar,
kept the attic clean & full of deep meditations.

The F.B.I. dropped by too,
shiny shoes & twin dark business suits,
skinny ties, smooth guys —
flashed ID asking me at the door if
Jim Thurber was around the premises —

naturally I'd never heard of the cat. They left
business card. "Give us a call if you see him."
That business at Laredo on the border
still haunting us.
Time was up. We were leaving.

New Year's Day we left for Big Sur. I had to dry out.
Susan came too, the baby growing inside her.
The morning we left I sent Peter Kocal sprawling
against the wall o.d. on wine & a hit of smack I gave him.
Pay back for what happened in Mexico.

I talked to Bill the night before about hot-wiring
the still intact Olds in the garage. We had to leave it
behind—tried everything to get it started.
Coming home late the next night our McCallister squat
was locked up and boarded all around.

On the last morning, junk sick,
we threw firewood and broken crates
into the trunk of Bill's old Falcon
& took off South. Shaky & stopping
along roadside to vomit in dewy coastal wildflowers.
Stopped again at some doughnut shop outskirts
of Santa Cruz, try to get a milk shake down.
70 miles South we got to abandoned cabin Big Sur,
eleven miles up Garrapata Canyon. No car, few clothes,
some blankets. Bill drove off, promised he'd return to help
us. We were convinced then we'd
never go back. Rent strike of '67 –'68.
End of a life.

McAllister St.

How to say something between spaces
inspiration dead like winter
inside a jewel which dreams
a name for a city, a maiden
beautiful, gift. Swirls of blue
exploding, snow blindness, diamonds
I'm helpless except love a space
holds me mute, ripples of failure
swimmer through deductions, injections
prisoners, threats, noise of this
rented room in our hearts hiding
too many excuses to remember
the door opens again, our love suffers
the plague black and white wants
goofers owes me five dollars
sells a highly advertised product
mixed with strychnine a specific
cure for errands and memory

2.

If only you could understand
I can't remember how to say
your name at night over & over
again locked all the way into you
arms legs belly woman mother
my care will not be enough for.
The rain weeps in my head
flowering with fear of it all
night repeating itself faster
light barely a space, something
someone said, is saying now.

1984 Page St.

Our uneasy reunion brings us
back, Big Sur to San Francisco
a city in ruins—1968. The freshly
painted room we rent lights off
drips cockroaches like hail,
rain down from ceiling
onto baby's crib
drop on her eyes crawl
across her face scurry in armies
across the floor over our blankets
In the morning
we leave without stopping to pick
up our rent from a landlord we
won't find for days.
Down Page St. another apartment
we get the top floor, roomy
sans roaches, curtains blow in framed
french glass doors around the turret
out onto fire escape. The baby is safe.
          Strung out again I plan reasonable amounts
to stay sane, slow the growing blue track
down my arm, play the music low under
dim yellow lights wonder at rented apartment
just below us. Never a sound or a voice
no chair legs scraping on floor. I want to
"borrow some sugar" visit our neighbors go
downstairs to say hello. To find out.
The door's ajar
          I see three leather-clad men still wearing
their shit-kickers asleep on single
pages of newspaper on bare
linoleum floor. There is nothing else
no tables, no chairs no beds, empty.
Only the gas oven door flipped
down the room dense with heat

A surreal life grows around us.
The tap water grows infection around
my mouth. Serious enough we go to
nearby Catholic hospital, nurses aghast
our tatters, their touch, concern give
penicillin I dream of moving in.

2

Second scene, unexpected actors appear.
Notorious Sergeant narc sweeps in through
fire escape door with his dim partner
takes a look around, lights cigarettes
asks us inane questions obvious, thrown
off by innocent hippies.
Susan sits across ready
spoon & syringe on coffee table
hides it crosses legs
turns slightly to answer
their stupid questions.
They exit the same way out window
down the fire escape ladder

That night we hear terror screaming
stairway light bulbs shattering
a man crawls toward us upstairs
to top flight against our door
jerked back by hair I'll cut your ear
off cocksucker rolling back down stairs
they've got him now dragged into ground
floor apartment to devour

We grab baby in blanket
run down blind stairs in darkness
past desperate howling
out to street, run toward friend's place
anywhere the fear our hearts
beating like drums banging what

innocence we had left about this
once shining city withered dry
overgrown now by poisonous weeds
rooted in the soil of evil.

The Scales

Eye to eye
on the scale our
eyes on the balancing
of things to
an exact weight.

Right now
a lot depends on
who measures best

Scales no pendulum
swinging or seesaw
violently going
up and down

Tapping easy
weight calculates
future limbos, confusing

dreams, photographs,
love in each of us
measured in this kitchen

trees framed in windows
light falling on another
amount tapped out for
sale, chance, change,

debt or fortune
the scales tell us either
not quite enough
or too much.

A Walk in Golden Gate Park

A walk in the park, sing
someway out of feeling—
afternoon colors bright pallor
of daughter's skin
don't allow myself words
I'd never say anymore
too gone on a frenzy always
leaves me a ghoul lisping
in imitation near daybreak bird calls
pierce inside say that I can't anymore.

Taking a deep breath to begin
holding it a foot twitching turned
toward immediate pleasure
dissolved in tablespoon
recurring dream of
drowning man his doubtful
salvation a bag of love &
a bag of death coming to save him
above

Living in Golden Gate Park

Stay with what you love
leave what you didn't
call no one to you
man or meaning

Instead, surround with strong arms
invisible auras make us plant or animal
growing placid, wild & beautiful
by moment. Depart any lie
that lets you keep your place.

I'll put no roof over your head
but this: the stars at night
a bed woven with stems & leaves

grass and feathers to sleep on
our warmth on a mattress of
our smallness and skin.

And may I at last
not mark you with unhappiness
but heed your gentle words
slow to open and be heard.

Sculpture at the Museum

She turns on the pedestal
balanced—her feet Rodin like
The muscles of her arms of clouds
holding out the real pink miniature
saint baby above her head
for all to see and adore. Her white buttocks
stretch to idealize Motherhood across centuries
of evolving cultures conditioned by her
now dripping beehives of breasts bursting
through latter day modern brassiere burnings
letting everyone know that she also appears
as a wild two-headed multiple-armed Kali vegan
religiously concocting multifaceted herbs
an incomprehensible predestined omniscient
life force with painted Karmic toenails rolled
to her new museum & trundled through
the Haight Ashbury on view for the wowed-out
ecstatic skinny youth long hairs with their guitars
& poetry acid & weed & absolute belief that we
could change the world beware all critics your hair's on fire!

Walk Away From It

(for Lew Welch)

How can you call yourself a city sometimes?
You've got your dirty moods your dark side
You're cruel & you know it
You're not a city right now you're a monster
Put together in Frankenstein's lab,
Idyllic to monstrance, attending surgeons Kali Yuga
Milarepa's cave of demons with surgical instruments
They might as well have used a bat cave for a model.
An ideal metropolis you ain't.
When they got done with you & scuttled off
an open-skull brain probe
had to be done before you terrorized
what citizens were left. Inside,
they found a fatty, concrete mass
with asphalt boiling up through
a gigantic malignant fissure.
Zombie-like cells morphed into
tentacles gone wild down
blood-shot streets. Your face
looks like curds of globular jelly
your eyes flash snakes of light,
writhe over deeper shadows,
gas everything with vast paranoia
occupy all parking spots inducing
fatal despair among auto slaves.
In order to stop flat lining
your surgeons try to scoop
out the soupy scrawl, burn
their fingers. Hot City! Inhabitants
heading for the exits; "The rest
of the team can close up."
Diagnosis: Wired to melt humans
down to slag as long as it lives.
Treatment: Consult Welch, et al.
1968 — Citizens aware of the problem

should walk away from it. Theory:
Small parts of it will die if they're
not around feeding it anymore.

Again

Love lights up my life like a flare.
Ten years ago a light fell on my head.
The knife of love split my heart like a ripe melon.
Not yet a man I trembled in the dark of her room.
We touched and died and gave ourselves to each other
For the first time. Loved killed me and I was transformed.
I tried to follow her and became lost.
Like a ghost locked out of my body
I waited in the cold. When she came back
I was the shadow of a lunatic mad with drugs
And paralyzed with fear.

Now ten years have come and gone
And what I had forgotten they could ever bring
Arrives again. You broke the locks on the doors,
Turned my desk into a garden. The hearts inside
The days on the calendar start to beat
Waiting for your pen to write across them.
Our hands touched. We looked into each others
Eyes and saw our desire like a deep pool
In the river at summer. I kissed you, your mouth
Was oil and honey ripe with promise. My heart
Went numb. Arrows of pain and heat went through
My body. I've lost control and forgotten God's laws.
Heaven is so far off. I see only your face
And your body when I close my eyes. A new road
Appears before me. Directions arrive with our letters.
Disaster glimmers like a forbidden enchanted city
In the distance. Your fragrance has burned itself
Into me like a radiation that leaves your essence
A taste on my tongue that never goes away.
In the morning I see my wife and children
Their eyes red with crying.

Roof Top

10:10 am.   beautiful sun
          daytime haze over bay

        The City ta ta

all laid out in neat little rows, fiery windows across bay
        tiny spots floating around — way down there!

drop ten capsules 00 dried peyote   HIGH CITY

drop 450 mg of lysergic acid, bathtub variety   HIGHER CITY

INSANE CITY!

hear it go woof woof

            ★

Of course,
        a herd of people
come out on the roof right when I'm having a good time

one of them has gone the wrong way &
runs around shouting "You're all liars, cheats, fakes

Phoneys."   {we're all standing around
          giving each other
          those creeepy looks
          saying "I don't know"

but "we know."

        Creature?

        I'M RADIANTLY IMBUED
          WITH EVERYONE I KNOW
               (drug experience, zen?

MUG SPOT   O GYPT
                              damn!   shower room of wars, gloom's
                                            (temporary, will pass
the whole mad thing about knowledge some mad
          with the love of it
                              (won't
                                    mention names

Here comes RA!
          holding court on the roof

boy, these scene changes dazzling
                    he's saying something about the peacock miasma body
you can imagine the color & the eyes
now his soliloquy on form being the MYSTERY
FORM playing with itself?

          apparently my name is Prakriti
                                    (tight rope walker from India?

          ★

RA orders some phenomena sports, he's big on these things

lots of play
          the young lord full of
                    good grapes
mystery tennis
          back & forth, no net
male & female yin & yang *(clichéd to death around here*
          heaven & hell *(Blake was good at that*

I'm worn out   can't he go back to Egypt?

I found some mushrooms growing in the shower

Mountains & Rivers

Yosemite Weekend

Third day on trail
morning parting w/ friends
under ominous sky

Jobs call them home.

Five miles later
walking alone
only breath & mosquitoes
punctuate rhythm of my feet
rising and falling
one in front
of the other
they find a groove
untie my mind
let go

Nothing but a vacuum
cleaner

Sucking up thoughts
through never-ending hole
Bowl
filling up constantly
emptied again

Christians pray without ceasing
Ave Maria   Others chant Om no hyo reng ge kyo
could chant
Coca cola Coca cola Coca cola
It's all the same!

Don't let the bad thoughts in
or let them in
& Buddhist watches tip
of nose
follows breath silently

inside out
human breath playing tennis
with itself indistinguishable

Changing point of breath
flow in
out in   out
ah.

Passing a swamp
mind off leash
feet taking care
of themselves
it's all together because
it's UN-together
        no mind no feet no me
Mr. Pure Perception:
all tree
all tall thin poised green reed
all mosquito zoom
natural bomber
all tree bole goiter hallucinating all

Message from the mind out enjoying itself among cloudy
peaks:

'Watch where you're going Thurber
before you fall in the lake'

II

Lost
down Ilhouette Creek
a mile into
bad brush
trail peters out.

'That couldn't have been the trail.
So what? It was a beautiful creek.'

I wasn't talking to myself
I was talking to the trout.

Two hours later
hot noon sun
double back over ridge
puffing
to Nevada Falls
I deal my feet out
like cards
flup flup flup
in the dust
ten miles to go.

★

Merced River trout
hypnotize me
lazy mirrors
coding sun darts
back from glass water
slivers of silver
    gone
in flick of tail
blink of eye

★

Over Mono Meadow trail
Big Vision hits me!
Re: freeze dried food

John Muir's probably
rolled over
& groaned He of the single fur coat wrapped around him
dead of winter

Latest backpack camping
expensive tourist
state-of-art bags tents stoves shoes bug repellent

YOU CAN GET RICH TOO — SELL FREEZE DRIED
CHRISTMAS TREES
in polyethylene huge bags
you stand up inside yr shower
fill with hot water
let soak 5–10 minutes
PRESTO
Authentic year round
Sierra Christmas
tree.

★

Glacier Point Trail
looking back
Nevada Falls
watch ghost white-maned
water drop lemmings
plunge
aerate
water droplets separate
    fall
re-form again in river below

all the same water   (water all the same)

Up the North Umpqua

Gravel-voiced the river whispers
Dawn breaks
log trucks
slide down
highway tube

Jake brakes
rupture dream birth-sacs
mind fills
   up
      to
Right here
Right now

Out window

river

a bird flying
wind
silk voice
    talks low
        echoes in sleep
our hearts

Daylight

deer float down hill
browse river's edge
Mergansers   Canadian Geese
Gray Heron
Water Ouzel   otters
show themselves
lone salmon slips
along narrow gravel trail
underwater   shadow

Osprey wheels
    turns tight
            circle
spots movement
then like a flashing knife
dives   a bolt spears
a tiny smolt

This opening of ourselves so vast
Our graceful life in nature, a paradise
accepted & unearned

MOTHER

Mother Earth sings like a sad bird
Mother Earth's tears roll down like communists in a waterfall
The blood of Mother Earth squirts through papyrus skin
Trees grow out of Mother Earth's ears dirt between her toes
The Amazon is Mother Earth's vagina one boob is Arctic the other
                boob Antarctica
Mother Earth's bellybutton tropical equator
Tattoos cover Mother Earth's indigenous skin
Mother Earth is the Mother of all Mothers

Mother Earth's a bad idea for NAFTA finks in bottled boardrooms
Mother Earth has five windows, trillions of eyes
                watching dirty water
        watching shriveled testes
hanging from trees

Mother Earth gets cancer from gassy clouds
Mother Earth's birds can't fly her birds drop dead & fall out of the
Mother Earth drowning by legal paper cement shoes
        no life jackets

hordes of canned attorneys twist truth defend heartless
feelthy corporate molesters stop mute Mother Earth testimony

Who conspires against Mother Earth?
Who runs after vomiting banksters?
Who stole Her music bird calls gurgle of streams wind in the trees?
Who sleeps on Her pile of ashes burning Amazon lungs?
          International secret corporate bestial perverts want donkey sex
& endless wars
Give Mother Earth pollution boiled planet & final extinction

Mother Earth holds all babies with ribs sticking out
Mother Earth wants to sleep but they're clear cutting the forests
Mother Earth needs help because everyone has gone crazy
          Her exhausted defenders can't wait any longer
          Her exhausted protesters carry no white flags
          murder all journalists murder their voices murder
          their stories murder their headlines shut them up

Don't slaughter Mother Earth
Calling all Corporate Murderers to stop operating on Her
          Dry her tears & blood
Make Mother Earth happy! Let
Mother Earth dance & laugh! Let
Mother Earth suckle you!

Let Mother Earth throw off her veils again

Let her hair down & do the boogie woogie of the soil
Let her rumba with the rivers strip for the sky fox trot with fire
Let her sing in our hearts! Let her whisper in our dreams

Get up off of Mother Earth right now you mother fuckers &

          LET HER BREATHE!

River, Run

River, run
Run clear over stones into deep jade-green pools
River run, run.
River run along banks, wide open
Along the bent reed grasses, across cobbled gravel,
White, under dark green army of trees marching your shores
River run, now tumble foam-white
Plunging froth like manes thrown back over black rock shoulders
Running fast over steep, brown round-smooth cracks in ancient
Basalt ledge rock substrate
Sliding over ghost green backs of torpedo shaped fish
That ride in your airy, sunlit currents,
Then accelerating down around bends
Riding your own race track, miles to go
Yes, run river run

Going out of sight around long black pylons of firs leaning
Streaking past eddies, the foam like the
Exhaust of your perpetual engines
Your mesmeric speed, motion within movement
Ticking past time, your
Smoke of waters billowing through
October's reds and yellows, leaves drifting
Along your eternal green
As you go by roiling, rippling, boiling
Charging, twisting down rapids, waterfalls
Snakelike, dragon writhing, bucking, breaking apart again
Then calmer, widening, slower
Dropping into pools
Long pools one after another
Rain dappled now
Clear blue lost color
Closing beneath grey-silver clouds like an eye closing

A wink, night coming on when still you shall run,
Running black and phosphor
Blinking under moon and stars
Running, running, running
River.

Fall Against

When all else Fails you
Fall against what's left:
the stillness there at the center of dawn,
mist rises like thin smoke off the river.
The first flash of silver—
fish rolling along the black currents.

Just after the sun raises its head,
like a stealthy Indian hunter
squinting over the rock cliff,
the fish sink deep again, wary
of that tiny slit of light. Now
the river reflects itself, the rocks
on the bottom disappear, the deep holes
are dark, impenetrable. Fear overcomes hunger.
Their wild abandon set aside,
the fish wait out the light

Then, at dusk, the light escapes
the same way it appeared—in a time between two dots
on a stop watch that can't be measured.
An osprey launches
into a slow wheel overhead, her sharp
eyes looking for a telltale movement
breaking the river's surface.

The line yanks in my hand
hard, a last hungry trout
ripping the water, just before dark

Spin the Wheel

I want to sing like a drunken bird
I keep seeing bloody ants
exit the hole in my hand
I see trees out the window
I'm the five senses looking for the sixth
I have five windows in the room
I'm water flowing over rocks
I'm a tree
I'm a cloud
I'm a duck
I'm a beautiful cinnamon duck
I'm a merganser
I'm the tide
I'm the flood
I'm rocked to sleep
I'm the beginning
I'm the hungry counterpart of the sky
I'm tears and blood
I'm happy
I'm in hiding
I'm the bark peeled away
I'm the trunk of the madrone
I'm smooth in my human skin
I'm curved and sensuous
I'm the limb of a woman
I'm a glorious breath
I'm the river
I'm flowing past the window
I'm always listening
I'm a line
I'm dropping
I'm the other shoe
I'm an empty mind

God talks to me in my head
I can hear his faintest whispers.

Blues Muse

Listening to Eric Dolphy

What use Poetry
always of despair?
What use this beautiful flute—
Eric Dolphy to make me sad?
What use words
when they desert me
common as a lover gone
long ago? What use ghosts
of poets, shades of their
words echoing against
my walls of silence?
What asylums might I find
rest in, heart & brain
in ceaseless flight?

The Return

Gone from you once &
having left, been the one
to break the branch, how plot
some comic return—"I'm baaack!"—
arms full of groceries, festive balloons,
flowers or a wad of bills
slapped down
on the kitchen table.

You command my desire
hung up and hooked on my own ways
I waited so long all the plants died

O methedrine you flower of neglect
O ode to such odd dreams help me
I can't desert my dreams
real & pleasured as any flesh,
bone or tongue. In whose heart
is known any failure of accepting?

As in mine, morning opens my eyes.
I'm overdue by weeks, this anticlimax
no reward for her no punchline
that's ever heard.

"Life Is One Continual Round of Pleasure"

For Bobby Evans

Lonely me can't talk tonight
My blond valentine miles away
I can't lay next to her warm
body tenderness sweet
I can't enter her voice
ephemeral voice estranged tonight
limp telephone to my ear

This morning, beautiful letter
arrives with sad poem someone
met me on Haight St. 1966
walking past Blue Unicorn
home to empty Spaceship
climbing stairs to meet women or a fix
no venture of prophecy this day
of birth 31 years alive still
the tracks of the Beast climb my arms

Blues music playing but I want jazz
FM jazz on kitchen radio

I'll eat a bean, a peach, take an elavil
drink gin, cook TV dinner
eating while I wait does time
pass faster?

Everything arrives by voodoo
magic letters, phone calls
my connection, I have hour
& 1/2 to show up for salvation or

damnation it's up to the telephone!
It's a command, curiosity & destiny
spaghetti popping needles
into the foreheads of malicious violets
on the radio give me Charlie Parker
whose sacrifices were enormous
lampshades, hungry diabetic
ferns growing twenty minute reveries
where I pledge allegiance to multidimensional
unknowns with some "Quick Acting"
methedrine foot powders

Last night I scored the name
of a "croaker that writes"
from a man I just met
"Pick up Bobby & give him
a ride home" An edgy request
tinged by worry to help someone
from an old friend leading me
through an unknown darkness

So few who had even a car
I'm his last chance to get home

I drove the shadow
of a shapeless man dim
interior of night in car
who whispered to me
the name of a doctor who would give you
all you wanted jotted down
each visit on the little
blue prescription pad

Bobby's leaning on the bathtub
coughing up blood
the dark frames of glasses
shading the deep creases
in his face a story

the years of worshiping
a need that ends like this
body finally crumpled
a small shroud to fit
& later the unsaid eulogy:
Bobby Evans
he was a "stand up guy."

Peace

Apparently God falls
out of my head daily
the bread of dreams
I've waited for
debts & distractions
to be forgiven, I
wanted the Power
to resist temptation
the power to eat
the bread to sleep
with the bread
think like the bread

walking across the street
hoping for the money
to arrive
I lose the race
toward stillness
every tic in your
facial gestures
delivers me unto
evil thoughts again
helpless when you're
on top coming
down on my
life, harder & harder

when it's over
it's easier in the kingdom
to sit up, speak with power
shake hands with glory
roll over & play dead
Ahhhmen

Horn in the Morning

Horn in the morning why
am I dead in your soft love
brass melting my night long
thoughts, the small lists
of rats on a wheel to keep from
being smeared in mirror photo-still
remembering the pretense
giving me the energy; a
solitary knowledge of my arrival
to robot-hood; the hypocrite —
my shadow on the wall. So
wife by blind luck; love blinds her eyes
to this weakness for a fatal light,
a card, a door, dreams —
the ambushes of remorse
that cannot be repeated
even by lovers
who lie to one another,
the walls of self-exile jammed closer
by the stupid hand of Self
waving in spite / of
seeing this is our flesh singing
the shame of the waste of our lives

Thinking

Days of thinking like snow
falling and drifting;
the plan never complete,
buried by our hesitant love
blinding us in the cold
world, wife, friends
all to save their own
skins, a cruel test,
winter & cities. Jail
blowing towards us like
a wind. Or the hospital
with heat. No voices
or anything like that,
just fear and anesthetic,
turning away from the child,
infant, daughter, muse
Julessa, the name dreamed
and called from the void, the
father a double — on earth
and in heaven, flesh
and imagination.
The cold begins to crack
in on me, stupidity
like ice growing on me.
All of this failure & neglect
losing me in a storm
no love can stop

1967

To a Friend

You're hooked on heroin
crossed off everyone's list. So love
is dark grows darker blood rising up
the dropper, black rose mushroom
seen through the glass syringe
squeezed back into the vein

the relief you sought now
in your possession & we are left
behind. We don't answer the phone
because it might be you. Our feet
block the door when you come here
Our excuse is lame: "He's not here
anymore." This is the pestilence
we can do without no money
a jail cell ahead. Let us not descend
there O God thinking we wanted
to be such as as the strongest
their pain pledged to hopelessness
too far for you now
And we are left behind, alone
turning body to body
in the morning
sun pours across us through scars
of winter dirt left on windows
of a city that imprisons us
clouds of soot rain down on
the rooftops burying so many
of us in the night.

2.

Morning city a museum we ghost
through silently all geometry
& reflections precise in sunlight
looked at like a stark photograph —
extinguished streets of garbage
cigarette butts & concrete mausoleums
to keep alive I'd be hooked again
if something willed it, turn away from
mornings devoid of sadness though
I would follow you where ever
some god be willing.

New York 1967

How to Continue

after Bill Bathurst

We linger in the warm afternoon
of our flesh, slow and careless
together as old lovers as in marriage
and in health slow filled up
with our laughter the memories
of so many hazards to forget
death too far away & too near
yet this is forever this afternoon
the light of sun shining through
us bending me to myself binding
us beyond ourselves still
& simple as the sleep that follows
our fucking our bodies like
twin birds or moon in mirror
meshed with air & wings
sailing into surprise birth
unexpected flowers we see
the other side suddenly we make it
through the veil together
find Paradise is nothing that lasts
forever causing us endless smiles
feast of your skin darling &
your funny daughter my only
gift to you goodness of tender
me all this sun a few moments now
under motionless clouds knowing
the music will begin again
but not waiting for its omens —
dream crazed circus music merrygoround
we're mounted on mad swans
circling in opposite directions
to the tinny repetition gongs &
brass whistles waving goodbye

Night Jazz

Going Away

Then we
were two
gather

Now we
are a
part

You are
going.
Away?

slight
click
europe

for
ever if
I bore

you rowed
some
money

in a
boat
buried

your face
& floated
across

the sea
like
a cloud.

Press the Flesh

Now while the impression
is fresh, press to the flesh
but first flash to the past;
fresh flesh pressed fast,
flesh flash of pressed wish
impressed by the vast vision.

Last Words

These are the only instructions
you will be given:

Since a cold day no more
leaks into dreams than hell
does, ask yourself—

Did the seed scratch?
Did she speak?
Was there something
going on?

Listen for the cold
exclusions in her
crooked face. Now
the last step,

the binding down
of an airplane
deep in the heart
of Saturday night
gives you the
finished product.
Lit up by
the shiny armor

of the stars.

Scat Scan

six saxophones 3 trumpets three trombones six pianos eight basses a
      few b-52's
      bullet hole haywire future
      human voice supreme
          instrument

dumdumdumdeededadeedodidideedodo   da da
      belliupbaba belliupbaba baaa

dunt ta dunt ta dunt ta dunt ta dunt ta dudnt at dunt ta dudnt tan
      dudnt dunt ta
summertime groovin easy the golden loads of doves rise high you take
      it jack

bud bud di da   bud dud bao ba

        dibud da deebudda do
buddadddadd Yaaaadddaadddaaa ddaaaadad
      did did di da   do
   da
      da
  do
             duuuuuuuuuuuuuuuuuuuu
saturdaynight/sundaynight

To the Hotel Eddy

for Tony Williams

Rode with Portland Tony talking fast
to the kids in the back seat from Nebraska.
Picked us up at dawn on Haight St.
wanna score some pot.
"Just give us the money," Tony says.
"We've got to go in alone, you unnerstand—
the man don't trust anyone he don't know."

Leery from friend's tales returned home, burned
we have to drive fast making left turns &
right turns, crawl down dim back streets
to lose their thoughts in street names &
corners, buildings & darkened store fronts.

Finally parked on Turk around a corner.
Tony jumps out with their reluctant money.
When their attention lags in long minutes
I jump out & split before they see
exactly where I went. No matter—

The spades in this hopped-up lobby
wouldn't betray Chief Nelder & lose the business.
I'm putting in nothing to wager
but my neck on dim chance of bliss.
They take our money faster than a bank

cheap bulbs, winking corridors
upstairs in Eddy Hotel
where name whispered back hope
"It's Tony," & cracked stranger's voice
closes the deal—"This is good shit, man."

Under nodding light, ceiling rot &
doors clear as mirrors cracked
ajar & numberless each one open
to parimutuel hunches on how
Brown is running today.

Our bet is down & we hurry
our hicks clamoring in the lobby below
"We saw them come in here"
to passive clerk; whores laughing
them down & trying them as tricks
for any money they might have left.

Our horse comes to a boil
in the stall of a Ripple cap
galloping along track of a vein
straight home to heart.

I don't feel it & walk out
thinking I've lost again
when Brown meaning finishes
in a rush of sleek amber bolted
through the pack running in my blood

way out in front of me
I'm falling in hallways trying
to get up from god knows where
Pushed & pulled in bathrooms
shoved underwater & dropped
crawling to fire escape throwing
up luck I'll never remember.

Conscious at last propped on stairs
Tony reads Tibetan Book of Dead over me
smiles like ancient Guru I understand
at once is talking about nothing you can
hold on to long enough to name like racehorses,
humans & hotels torn down & vanished in Time
like the boys from the cornfields
tired after waiting six hours, gone home wiser
while we make it down fire escape in dark
to friend's pad around corner down on Webster St.
Yet pushed out again past midnight two hours
we nodded through unfinished conversations
& food they served us spilled & fumbled
fighting off dreams to sit erect & human.

"Pot heads are always so righteous," Tony says.
We weave toward my flat, rent unpaid,
where Tony won't be found one night at least,
his life all trails burned back to him
in alley or vacant lot, at night or broad daylight,
his head kicked in by motorcycle boots & pointed toe
patent leather street shoes.

Sky Ranch

Blue Clouds

borrow some face
row the land over
myself with a cloud
put down the dead burden
float down the deep grass
lay in the river
come back cloudless
in my borrowed mind
row a cloud across the land
now, now! a dead one says
to the dead ones
waving hello
to the live faces
as they float by love
as they float by.

Sky Ranch, Greenfield Village Inn

Walt Whitman I don't lament your lost America
I know you wouldn't, you'd dig these super-highways
eat hamburgers, play pinball, twirl the t.v.
Your soul was robust enough for anything, motels,
        used car lots, electronic meat brain
        spaghetti—
You'd weep for Kennedy the same as you wept for
        Lincoln
there was nothing skeptical about you

your joy in you in the moment

you were the future

Sky Ranch Sugar Cube

Looking at the woods
in four dimensions —
through, from both sides
above & below. Radiant
purple trees white-veined bark
standing in the gloom.
      Later,
Back at the cabin
      eating shiny
peas from a bowl.

LSD 1964

from The Book of Dead Indians

The Book of Dead Indians

It would have to be some Indian civilized enough—
americanized in whiteman's schools
speak English have whiteman's religion
in order to talk sentimentally like whiteman
about his death. But Billy Runs-like-Deer
is not like that. I don't know
what he was like, what he thought
or didn't think or what he felt in his heart
when they had him surrounded, when
the women and children were starving
when they had no moccasins standing
in the snow, when the bucks were up-tight
with a kind of resignation, ragged & hounded
in their bones, full of loose sounds
the steep mountains at their backs
when they knew the Great Spirit
was coming to get them when
seeing the winter sun for the last time
when remembering the moon they understood
they would never kill themselves like the whitemen
killed themselves in fear and terror
with Custer at the little Big Horn and now
when the sadness rose up in them like a black ghost
when they were having a last smoke
with the black Spirit Indian with the big wings.

Fort Klamath

"Do you want
the Indian version
or our version?"
The sales clerk trying
to be helpful
in buying a book
about the Indian wars.
It's 1977, a hundred years
since they hanged
Capt. Jack, the Modoc
peacemaker out there
in the cow pasture
fenced off with cyclone
wire & Closed for the Season
signs put up. All but a
handful of Modocs left.
The clerk tells us stories
about when the tribe
was terminated and each
Indian got a cash settlement.
How one squaw put in a
swimming pool next to
her trashed out single wide
& some buck bought ten
Cadillacs & drunk, drove
straight through the
showroom window. Says
now they've been "assimilated"
Now they're not even a tribe

Why Aren't We Happy?

Why aren't we happy now that the old life is gone, like some
forgotten relative that's passed
away? No more mainlines to the heart spreading a slow easing of nasty
fear, no more manic
white powders making you leap the moon & chatter to agonies in
heart at dawn in misbegotten
places. No more seething rides to strange cities of night only to return
broken again. No more
to push Love's face into the mud.

You Go Your Way and I'll Go Mine

I want you to leave with generosity
we can divide all that's left
which is nothing
with the pack on you can
carry enough to get you through
to the nearest Boddhisattva
whose Heart is like a Wheel
if you bend it you can't mend it
you'll pass the cows out
in their steaming colors of November
under the fog the night
the moon went out
these are the only instructions
you will be given

Trees Can't Talk

Oregon is some tired old whore
She's been around — they've been working
her hills 150 years
Her flaming green hair,
Hair of endless forests
Her green velvet body covered
with the sweat of
good ol' boys

That turned her out
Fucked her over
& under with thousands of
    clear cuts, gyppo loggers
putting it to her
Ploughing through her flesh

Her bark brown breasts, hills
of summer
Red mud of scabied
streams trickling
from her thighs
Bleeding, laid out on her
golden yellow buttocks of Autumn

The eye of the deer looks out from her belly-button

The black mouth of Chinook hides in her cunt

The sadistic cigarette burns of slash
healing over
pale green scars of second growth
Brush piles up for fires to burn her
  only
Salve of manzanita, juniper to heal

She's had a thousand
        chain saws rip her &
she's good for ten thousand more

Oregon bitch, all heart
You're sold cheap
by your pimps,
The corporate timber bosses &
sold out by your own body guards —

The United States Forest Service

Hibernation

Every winter I get the urge
to store up some fat visions
to sustain me through my not
believing much anymore.
It's hard to remember the dreams
I had during the slow restless sleep
that shut me down to barely breathing
blood chilled to slow ooze, hunger
gone, just enough of that fat melting
away until spring when I wake up
hungrier than hell for some flapjacks
bacon & eggs that I still do
believe in. I can't remember for sure
but it may have been the Dalai Lama
keeping me warm for awhile
in my cave & promising to
meet me for breakfast when I woke up.

               ★

Listen: Grey clouds, still leaves, no smoke
no wind, no cars, hazy hills covered
with yellow daubs of color scattered—
Oaks among the Doug Firs.

The Deep Sea

The deep sea
is a detailed
countryside of
eyes
speaking
in tongues

For Russell Means

Not all the poems about dead Indians
have been written. Not all the Indians
are dead yet. Then there is the problem
with all their horses & the half-breeds
& the 1/4s 1/8s 1/16s 1/32s & what
the speed limit is going to be on the rez.
In the bar some cowboy asks me why
did the chief let his sister screw a
Negro calvary man to create this "situuaation?"
Squaws were trained to just lay back and take it
to the bank—Under no account blame
the whiteman for coming—no fault of hiz.
There's nothing worse than a dead Indian
unless it's a drunk Indian. Sheridan would
subscribe to that. You can keep taking their
money & giving them misery. The Quick
Stop grocery store on the Rez in Browning
Montana leads the nation in per capita
package sales of beer but the 7-11 is putting
together a treaty to get in on it. The subject
of dead Indians hasn't been exhausted.
We could still elect one President.

End of the Trail

The systematic extermination the extermination
systematically carried out extermination
of the indigenous people systematically
the Plains Indians whose system
was in harmony with the earth the vast
plains the buffalo systematically exterminated
along with the peace pipe proffered
systematically by the increasingly baffled
hand that was systematically betrayed
by 400 broken treaties
sacred food source at first shared but
systematic conscious hate & unconscious
the system of sustaining native living
body & spirit harmony ten thousand years
before systematic invasive cancerous host
attacked the body of the Mother Earth &
Her Peoples, bio-regions the only body a system
one with itself which was inseparable &
the land & all that dwelt therein but Sheridan
himself a systematic kind of guy spoke up
of a system to "Let the buffalo hunters
kill, skin & sell until the buffalo is exterminated."
all 30,000,000 of them
& the Lakota's source of food clothing & shelter
was systematically removed from the system
so the red savages could systematically starve.
Before the Wild West shows Buffalo Bill
& his boys systematically cleared the plains
getting rid of that first great American nuisance even more
systematically lethal than the dawn raids on sleep
ing women & children & old men systematically
blown apart with artillery Gatling-gunned down
& finished off with repeating rifles tracked down
by the Indians called Judas scouts by Jesus's men.

Lightning Bird Sharks

Lightning bird sharks
on greased tracks Overhead, steel swims
through the air creeps of light
        traffic eyes   The moon is
            now divided between us
I know everything   I'm looking
    for a job

Star Shatters

mind   ocean   catches   star//
                    stretched to ocean by fire//
touches mind   ocean catches

        fire   star   & ocean speak

Ocean catches mind//

        shatters star   fire

catches fire

Ocean   touch   star   connect   fire   speak   mind   catches

        shatters

Dont Call Him Chief Fany More

dont call him chief fany more
        for there is no cheief
        WEEEEEEEEEEEEAJOBALONGOOOOHO HO HO
                    SESAME
                       !
OLD MUNGY LIPS ENTERS AND SAYS 000HALAAAH
        AAA HUUSMOCOCOCKLLLO

                            chef?

There Is Disbelief in the Stew

there is disbelief in the stew
there is nothing to write
now wouldn't it
start to now start
doing from the tips
of our blue wings
broken down too
now show us some
            stream of light
near the source
            the stone now
brought back
            to serious!
home now
you go

Limbs

        limbs
    broken from a
      tree huge
      eucalyptus

          leg
      expertly cut
      off placed in
        a box

      the secret
      inner life
      of a tooth

from The Book of Dead Radios

Radio R.A.G.E. FM

it's 1:15 am. Radio R.A.G.E. FM is on
playing continually in my head. I can't
turn it off. Voices talking: "Napalm wouldn't
have gotten them out of their holes today."
"We cut loose on those commie bastards...
man those dinks fought hard but we gassed
their asses." "More of them in the rice paddies."
"Then Winky showed up with ol' Willy Pete
and hosed them down. Jesus that shit just fries
the hell out of them." "Yeah." You 'member
when we used to toast marshmallows and they'd
catch fire and all the insides would drip out?
"That's just what they looked like — all fried
and bubbly and pink shit bustin' through. "Hey
what do you think that stuff is?" "They told me
it was a secret and not to talk about it." I heard
some brass say it was white fosforus. You think
it comes in all different kinds of colors?"

Vietnamese doctor says "... burning phosphorus
produces 800–1,000 degrees centigrade heat ... deepens
burn wounds ... generates great pain in nervous
system." U.S. spokesmen mouthpiece sez "We sure
are pleased with those backroom boys at Dow.
The original product wasn't so hot — if the gooks
were quick they could scrape it off. So the boys
started adding polystyrene — now it sticks like shit
to a blanket. If the gooks jumped underwater it
stopped burning so they added Willy Peter so's
to make it burn better ... even under water now. And
one drop is enough; it'll keep on burning right down
to the bone."

It's 10 to 4 in the afternoon. I'm still listening.
I have to listen. Some newscaster is saying 3
South V. farmers were gutted and hung from
the trees for "aiding the Americans." Maybe
the VC found a candy bar wrapper in their hut.

Hell no we won't go. There is no way, ever
in this lifetime or the next or the next that I'll
go to any of your wars, America. Everyday we're
sick to the heart, to the bone, wandering your streets.
America, what's wrong with you? Where is my land
of dreams, where is my home of peace and justice?

Where is there some invisible hand of pity or sorrow
to slowly turn off this radio?

3:15

the time is 3:15. the radio is not on loud
enough. heartbreak dead ahead. that big bluesy
sound. I have lain in bed two days, down with
heartbreak no. 25, the woodpeckers hammering
as I lay here, as I lay here with nothing — saying
it and this is to be called poetry   god —
dammit don't you understand. it's all over.
poetry is all over. listening begins

car sound   , wind; paper flutter,

        radio   .   ain't it peculiar,   who

will not tell:: every-thing
     thing is
          poetry   from the left to the right right
to left, up   side wards   ,   backwards.

"all of you who bought the poisoned cheese from
Safeway, please return it to the store you
bought it from"   .   Nothing more than nothing

can be said, emptiness is the form, continuity
 the poetry   itself

Somebody's Talking on the Telephone

somebody's talking on the telephone
downstairs t.v. sets are talking out of their minds
the dead radio on the table suddenly comes to life
I picture myself walking through the tea garden instead of going there
Is there no progress? Is this all a big drag?
Will the nations of the mind make peace?
Will this long conversation on the phone with her
enhance my chances of making it with her
before the army gets me? Before we're dead?

laundry hangs white pink blue & red in afternoon
shadow on back side of the building
yellow roses high on their weak heads, long stalks
magnolia
I'm always looking out into back lots
of somebody's pad

I'll give the sad sexual ghost of her
the pair of ear rings
that nobody could wear without pierced ears

Vietnam dangles like a bloody ear ring from the pierced ear
of America

The Moon Chants Down on Me Naked

The moon chants down on me naked
in that eye these years kept me here
in adoration of myself the youth
lying on the grass Buena Vista park
eye lids light with drugs
ephemeral Frances I love asleep
      drunk
with time my hand rests
around her shoulders

The moon joy cast down on me invades belly
of ME
no hand on my belly horror of war

I'm not going shove your war don't call
my number I won't answer fuck you bastards
which way Canada I'll drop acid
put on warpaint hand out peace leaflets
claim I'm gay go to jail go limp carry banners
chain myself to Dave Dellinger & Joan Baez
break out your grimy windows Oakland Induction Center
torch your shoestrings wear a black beret I'm not kidding
about killing my dad marrying my mother you Army shrinks!
Who wants to help you spew out flaming body parts
kill yellow people brown people red people black people?

I'm sick of jet bombers & helicopter sperm shooting
napalm thatched huts nutty invisible war hand rattling
my windows goosestepping out of T.V.'s jesus I can't
stand it anymore when will it end? I'm sick of it
pour out some blood on the bibles for me Berrigan, LBJ
do something! Trash bin McNamara Rusk Kissinger
Draft them! Make them pull the triggers

This Poem Should Remind

This poem should remind   you
of nothing   ; though it   is
something, going in, like a radio
tone to your head,   it still   should
remind you of Nothing

   'all the somethings in the
world begin to sense their at-one-ness whensomething happens
that reminds them of   nothing.'

The Modern Way of Doing Things

the modern way of doing things
modern way,   one must know about
time
interval
silence
syllables
sounds
words
meanings
listening
acceptance

& the presence of mind not to
back the car into her garage door

What brings order in the world
is to love and let love
do what it will

We're Advised to Go Straight

we're advised to go straight
past Go   collect millions
of laughs, grope the strait-jacket
police, spill our pills on the
bare ass come spit lick that old
hack

     I BELIEVE IN THE MAGIC
WHICH SETS US ALL FREE

You are now all free

REGARDLESS of the rise/fall
of your ephemeral

help nite parachute blood space
mama yelling for touchdown

mayday swim guitar spurt nightfall

What Have I Left Out Mother?

what have I left out mother?
that it is not all dancing?

now every noise is in its place

cold tea and the golden gate bridge.

There is a knock on the door.
There is nothing like

a licorice airplane flying

Difficult Keys

difficult keys
        largely
waves and lips   leaping
lips leap
 jazz   incomparable pink-tight
         ass   going away   fast

  on the back of a motorcycle
  whee, she shouts back at us

  disappear
d is a p pea ring
on the back of night/

Eyes

eyes
        decadentmeaning
        air
        morning gobblepick

       ★

        apologiesteeth
              twilight
        sting/
           beak-king, fang-rot
        pant

Be Kind to Yourself

I demand Everything that sits, stands, walks swims, flies, sees
      or hears
Explain God to the radio! Suck gas from the galactic zoom
      heat moon
I say love yourself in deep rumba pure knowledge of your only body
      Here & Now!

Joyous Youth Forests

joyous youth forests
longing, kept pets two-fisted tobacco chewin' homosexual
        bisexual
  heterosexual
        on legs?   not ashamed?

  Et tet tet tet tet tet thettetttattettte
        machine gun?   Rose?   Sperm flute?   Herbie? Mann
        coverlet under
together/nightsleep

Inroads

inroads love-fog   ROSE   ROSE   ROSE sun-god
old bosoms   breasts giodarno please (ape logos ies   Chris/
        sakes!
      first of it
fingers, multicolored
Buds BUDS BUDS!!!   bungalows,
stone breasts   tears

Animals/

animals/

        essential vegetable screwup nightlegs whore-man,
          thought,   suck

        environmentmineralatomic
        rustoscillation   veins

/vain/

On the Arizona Method

(after Film Noir)

In Arizona,
they puts bodies in the brush
where they thrown and won't be found
except by helicopter
or the hound
and first by hares with noses
twitching of night.

What desperado
con on the run
jealous spouse's
hired killer or rage
of mental defect would
cause such slaughter
walk away, leave wallet
holding dollars?

Always,
stopping to pick up fatal stranger
asleep in roadside cars
changing tire
or out of gas
they clipped in ear
with the big clipper
of a tire iron.
How hefty! Cold.
And the Big Dipper,
above, more hefty
to our imaginary hand
than real headline stories
picked up from
newspaper stand

1964

Lamentations

Dawn

Dawn fades meaning
from our arms fallen
lifeless around each other.

Now daylight. Hours
later I'll come to you
for the last time

Wishing for that other
forgetfulness I purchased
at any price.

Morning

In this morning
Murder, away
from you away
from Sun pouring
over us through
winter scars—
dirt left
on windows

Away from
this city death
death of its death
gleaming mad
imprisonment clouded
with soot losing
from our sight
so many friends
in the night

The Usual Too Much

the black puddle blinks
      back my face
      from
   the black mirror

        perfect reflection!

(showering spray of light!)

        TV
transformed into buzzing thunderbolt god
bathroom exploding in light

Marilyn Monroe assures me that
      "This should be enough"

The window yawns open
perfect lipsticked lips of night
         appear

Lament

So only in secrecy like rain
forgetfulness like surf repeating
dissolving & reappearing

      The clouds
explosions stacked up
            over the city

An airplane drones in the blue
loneliness of Absolute Sky

through the hole
          in the wall
of a word
        see

Stainless turn-on fang & blood
venom & adrenaline goof
          Circus nods & sleeps

a thousand mosquitoes flash
          needle sting

& I lay me down to poverty
back in America lay me down
to bedlam down to crazy
down to nightmare

species of a bad dream

The Mistake

Our mistake grown
wide enough & healed
now to permanent scar
between us the dead space
of ghost-white skin
shrinks to memory

leaving nothing
more important
than hurrying
to you, clouds
never to part again
the way you once

passed over me
a forgotten debt or
gift with strings
attached, you're
that free pass
misplaced somewhere,

unused a year ago
still haunting
my empty wallet
& I keep going
through yr signals
jaywalking across

unchanging lights
of our lives
for whose sake
I risk the traffic
reach the other side
the lights unreadable

in the afternoon
glare of red, yellow
green like meaning
that fades from our arms
empty with fatigue
of worn out dreams

Awake all Night

dawn pulls shrouds
across my eyes
heavy without sleep

I survive the daily
timetable with promises
unkept, our meetings

missed by watches
late or stopped
we pass clockwise

beneath the hands
of hours left
until the last

Love Potion

Love like some
familiar poison

the rain
the water
the dreams

the currents
alchemy of
your body

filling the dream
fills the heart
eats the poisoned

meat in my
heart is a
gorilla

Marriage

Time will tell
Time will tell
Time will tell

Time will tell
Time will tell
Time will tell

Time will tell
Time will tell
Time will tell

Seasons

When Gray Governs

"When gray governs it looks like fate."
But it's only the season again, an edge folded down
Since it's the same as last year we hardly notice the difference.
The old season slips away, goes to sleep or into hiding or mothballs.

I can't kid myself, it's always the accumulated lack of something —
our condition
that keeps me hanging on while everyone else is changing dance
partners
like mad in anticipation of the next tune of colors or changing lights.

It's blind luck when I feel good enough to look for a
mythical four-leafed clover or

swinging on a star goddammit, pushing
gray sky back and forth, shuttling like the weaver's loom
an old pattern on a new blanket woven of pure November.

April

The sun still comes by day to the unbeliever
His ear pressed to the magic silence
His eye at the keyhole of dreamy gates
His hand turning the knob of a strange door
His brain an abyss of weathered clouds
His tongue's an inconvenience of monosyllabics
His nose sucks in the perfume of dust piling up

Overhead, cold sun paints April blue
Puts the town on fresh spring ice green and blue
White clouds streaked with dirt hover eagerly
Like the dead for news that might wake them—
A breeze to pull them across the horizon

No act of mental will human belief or good cheer
Can start them on their journey

May

I'm lying on the couch,
My life's endeavors scattered on the floor.
White pieces of paper flapping &
Sprinkled onto the carpet of this room;
      Beat-up blue dictionary with black tape on the spine,
My empty chair in front of the typewriter —
An overloaded, unfinished pine-shelf bookcase against the side
                of the brick fireplace;
A make-shift desk covered with a jumble of fly tying materials,
The old wood-framed photos of the Oregon coast
           in the style of Ray Atkinson
                on the walls.
A plain dresser with more books on it.
My eight-foot long narrow desk dead ahead beneath the window,
Two cheap Japanese prints on bamboo hung on both sides.
The knotty piece of driftwood on the sill.
The big madrone outside the window in front of the fir.
The corner of the old cabin's roof over the desk.
Loose strings on the rainbow colored mobile fluttering in the breeze.
The roar of the river —
And if I stood up and looked out,
The river itself, never-ending, rolling away
In white and green noise.

Summer

Ha Ha I am Master of the Hammock,
levitating over the back deck above the brown estuary.
A warm breeze kisses my lips,
a warm tongue is licking my eye lids.
My body aches with emptiness.
The book of the Heart Sutra
slides off the hammock.
The tide slips in effortlessly,
imperceptible to most. Right now
I see everything, the dark green water,
rotting pilings, fir trees crowding the water's edge—
patient Blue Heron fixed like a statue
in the shallows, bent over, long beak, eye cocked
for the tiniest movement of a tiny fish underwater.
Right now I hear everything;
A Mourning Dove's plaintive call, unrequited.
Right now I taste the ice tea in the tall green glass
Right now I feel the warmth of the dog nestling next to me
Right now I'm empty
Right now I'm a mirror showing only blue sky
Right now the mirror is empty
Right now the mirror shows "I don't know"
Right now there is no mirror
Right now there is absolutely nothing
Right now the dove coos again,
I've never heard an answer
All summer long.

The Moon and I

The moon and I aren't friends
since it failed to drive me
crazy. Now I look at it,
a cold coin swelling
up over the Panhandle,
seducing eucalyptus
to heavy-rooted dances.
Traffic flicks down Fell St.,
rows of lights,
rubber-tired swishing moans,
throats of adoration
for the moon. The moon
goes up on edge and rolls
straight west out over
the ocean and sinks
like an iron grapefruit.
Some nights I can see your face
and some nights I can't.
That is the pleasure of the moon.

1965

1970—1990s

Hunger

Hungry for the word it might be
libelous swinging through the trees
in search of a pantomime of shadows
sweetening the river while my hands
sleep, upturned on their sides, palms open
like mouths snoring incredulity at their labors
which never had the chance to be
"limited to the desire to set down something
as it passes" instead they've been hardly
noticeable as light as light moved
the speed of thought did what
they were told before being told
what to do — Oh how hungry I am!
And that the hands, my hands could
reach inside like those of
a Filipino faith surgeon & lift out
hunger & desire like the chicken
guts in the color photos on the cover
of the evangelical magazine
it never ends wanting to read the words
wanting to sing the words, take a shower
in the words Be the words, have someone
say oh you make the words? Oh I am
words falling asleep on the typewriter
hands snoring fingers closed like eyes
whistling in the dark

Domestic Astronauts Blues

Searchin' through the shambles
of my heart's twisted mess
we're all so much less
for all that's left of us

Our millionth dream shot
just another ring
around an empty cup.
Love can't cook up

no medicine to shoot
us very far
Your blond anger
caused our launch to flop.

Now I'm crawlin round
the ground trying to apologize
My solid fuel of feelings
didn't homogenize.

My rocket jockey's shot
fizzled into sound
of scribbled madness
fell back into the Gulf.
Control complained "It's hot!"

Execs tell news
it was expendable
Write it off as dues
tax loss donated

non-refundable to
my heart fund.
Doctors can't use sugary
words in surgery

on two open hearts
tryin' to replace elastic
with something plastic.
Wives are tryin'

to keep from hatin' us
& friends assigned
to pick up the pieces
of her kite & my model kit.

This is the taxed-out
love payer's broken hobby
somebody's got to knit.

Adult Child of Alcoholics

Mother trained me with whips
& curses. Not of the dark
but of the terrible ways of
coming apart at the center. I felt smaller;
at night the jungle came alive.
In the blackness before
the stars took my breath &
animals & insects started talking—
It was their loud crazy talking
that filled my heart with distances
& something else, nothing
that you could ever name.

Finding Your Voice

(for the Academy)

A man stooping over to pick
up nothing visible to me
holds it out in empty hand—
"Is this your voice?" he says.

I could tell he wasn't joking
because he was dressed in all black
or white, perhaps he wasn't dressed
at all—he was serious!

In yr case, he goes on,
there's usually a clue—
it's a pattern in those one-
of-a-kind things. Unique
original raspy formulations.

One broken egg
in every carton one slice
bread with mold & one
unidentified severed head
in El Salvador. Perhaps
your own non-existent voice,
he says, laying there on my
fingertips, reminded me of
palm readers fingertips
accurately read my future
mistakes now that he didn't
have to hold them there was no
mistake—supposedly it was
"my" voice started talking
as usual wouldn't shut up

the world is mad yes I'd said that
many times over people were
sick of hearing about
dark interior regions brooding
intentionally words lunatics
in asylums jump onto pages of my skin
writhe like black snakes of ink tattoos
memory pictures earth can't reason
so gone night clouds lights coming
on across the water way the hell
over there I hold my breath counting
not being the same over here I can't tell

old man trying to hand me bogus voice.
I ask him is this some fairy tale,
bad joke or emergency plan, he says
shut the fuck up you & your fake voice
"Is that the only one you can think of?"

A Story About Nothing

I heard the ocean last week & tomorrow I'll hear
wind & rush in to turn off the threatening chorale
of voices on the radio. I plan to keep pulling elusive
threads unravel endlessly I'll smile the same way
my face opening & opening, Wonder Morning awake!
o yee fog slide over easy to feel foolish trying
to hold it back gather it into my arms one sentence
takes hours don't you think? Mouth opens again
& again nothing comes out driving home luminous clouds
paint brush Sistine sky chapel ceiling dome above brush
strokes pure moonlight miles away farmhouses sprinkled
electric bulbs across hillsides I know the cold
straw filled barns where new lambs burrow
under ewe's bellies suckle night long winter dark
driving darkness past wind & time crossing
rivers silence traces a geography of scars
trying to remember something true to yourself

Jump Start

In my dream I'm not dreaming.
My dreams are inside a dead
battery under hood of shadowy car.
I'm trying to jump start the battery
turn over the dream engine
but nothing happens. I see
my hand pick up the positive
jumper cable. It's a red snake shrieking
happy danger: "I am," it shouts
"You are," "It is!" "Everything will
be O.K." "Life is Good," "You'll be
happy, rich & famous." "You will never
have to work again!" The red snake
makes positive statements. I pry open
its jaws & snap them shut around
the {+} marked battery terminal.
Positive to Positive.

The dream revs up behind my eyes:
I'm a rich Arab, white turbaned
wearing striped bathrobe & pajama bottoms,
sporting silk slippers at the Oasis
leaning against my Rolls-Royce under the palm trees.
Positive to Positive.

Now the dream coughs & sputters
without warning, stalls out
In the next dream I don't want,
The one where my hand grabs
the other cable, black & cold,
stiff like a gun barrel pointed
against the {-} marked terminal
of blackness. Negative to Negative.
I see my severed head strapped
atop a black box attached
with strings of wires. It's a coffin
of dead dreams. I watch

my mouth open trying to scream.
No sound comes out.
Negative to Negative.

　　　　rising & falling
winking in their course
　　　far out
　　　on the floating black sea

Out Into Idaho

In the clouds
above the desert
Dumbo, assorted Schmoos
& Miss Piggy float
on their backs
or slide on their bellies.
Father Time, naked
to the waist, beard
hanging down &
my own face, blown up
dangling a fetus body
watch space pigs snorkeling
toward open-mouthed
demon-dragons.

A sky gallery of stuffed
animals & cartoon characters
hanging motionless over
perfect knob cone pine Christmas
tree farm outside Bend, Oregon
deep volcanic Cascades breathing
in snowy distance alabaster
beneath fluted light.

2.

& Hosmer lake, my own
beautiful Hosmer
with Kerouac's Hozomeen mountain
looming over — ospreys fall
from pine perches, showoffs
strafing shallows for juvenile
salmon, hit the water like
fat kids doing cannonballs
& red-epauletted blackbirds
chasing, courting & yellow-
headed brown birds & great
solemn crane slowly
raising a right foreleg lumbering
off into thick reeds

Tenderloin Hotels, San Francisco

Buzz of
refrigerator
breaks into

dreams of
room in
the Hotel Zena,
the Hotel Fulton.

Welfare hotels
in North Beach:
The Hotel Eddy
The Hotel Wentley.

Lea's Sleeping
Rooms, 3 days.
Places I went

away to kick

To the Smokers

Marijuana, weed, grass, pot
green, Cannabis, Bueno, La Mota—

Greetings that brush against my heart
like a wing changing my direction
suddenly through the sky's Mind, Being
miraculous relief so dreams come

as sacred & awaited
cramp & spasm of muscles
surrender to pull of aching delicious
now.

Caretakers passing me joints
in the kitchen.

How my tortured velocity shook
the walls. That rigor mortis of remaining
myself

opening naked now
in slow morning

Sixth Street

Like vampires we rouse ourselves at dusk;
obey the imperial hour of our
need. We make our way
into the city's night, across
Market St., turn onto Sixth, looking
to score, wait for the man who said he'd
meet us here at 10.

Here such misery—no where to turn away.
Empty shells once human,
still alive, drift in madness,
lurch down alleys wearing rags
of filth under dim neon shadows.
Cockroaches and rats hide
in liquor stores, pawn shops
and corner groceries. Everything else
locked up, windows barred & chained.

Here the great jaws of some hungry god
gouge light from men's eyes,
scatter it back over dark streets,
rain down cruel misery without
reason. Swollen skin, blood-veined eyes
open sores, rotted teeth, stomachs
bloated, ulcerated; only pain their bosom friend.

A man like a seal pushes himself
along on mechanic's dolly with
his stumps working like fins,
a quarter between his teeth to buy one more bottle
of Thunderbird in corner grocery.
We walk up Sixth then down Howard.
My mind turns off, overloaded by this torture
beyond any reason.

We shuffle past the Howard Hotel, ship
from hell, slave cargo of rotting men stagger
under naked bulbs, radiator steam heat.
Sweat stenched walls hold the smell forever.
"They sell you anything you want
or can imagine in there," Bill says.
We move slowly past Act I theater—
skin flicks—old woman buys

ticket for all night warm place.
Men in rumpled suits come out
sweaty, "After a while it gets
monotonous," one says.

No sign of our man. Time is
running out. Circling the block, the last corner
a Rescue Mission painted red.
A Cross adorned with light bulbs. Free meal
and a cot. A long-hair bums a cigarette
from the preacher, bullshits him
before the sermon.

Our man doesn't show. Another sleepless
haunted night bereft of drugs to soothe
my fear, stop this pain my body can't endure
alone; the lack of love, someone to touch,
or taste the water of meaning on my parched tongue.

from The Book of New York

Again

I could think for a million years
when the dawn arrives
& the birds start talking in my head

I'd laugh two
times, once with fear

once with something else.

Love Poem

Everything is just as it should be,
Not the way I wanted it.
Much lower. Last choice
As a matter of fact.
I wanted a bicycle for Christmas
But got a pair of socks & an orange.
I'll never play Christmas
With them again. Pocatello, Idaho
French amphetamine & no destination.
No identity. No feeling. If I were
A vegetable & you were crazy
Would you marry me anyway
Would you have my Karma?

October opened

October opened
the letter of a gray
day outside
the yellow post office.
Slit a cloud open
tore a ragged edge
pulled out a free
offer.

JIVE

Woman you must be crazy
Thinking about going
After all I've done for you

I Have Seen Women in the Clouds

I have seen women in the clouds
three days passing, green
flame striped mermaids on Tuesday
Wednesday she's rolling over
in her silver threads across
the bed of a silk horizon
arching white against blue
sheets, her pearls of heaven

but tonight it's two women
leering, their horrible mouths
open in anticipation of kissing
Mother good night, mother
with her handlebar mustache
frowns & winks & (merges,
Poof!) with the Renoir woman
in the punched-sleeved dress
fanning her spurs over open
pits, riding her lucky duck
straining to leap into the open
mouth of a headless
astral-headed gander!

Christmas Away from Home

for Shar

A communal feast
for a pad full of junkies
who've all gone out to score.
Shar & I left in the empty
flat to finish the decorations.
I stand on the table reaching
to hang a final star or mistletoe,
her arms around my legs
to keep me from falling.
For a few seconds a warmness
of desire climbs & pulses
through my body. I want
to slip down into her arms,
empty myself of fear at last.

Ray & Bill return, the others
drift in. The smell of turkey
baking. Some twinkling lights,
mistletoe & tinsel hung
in the windows. Bebop
on the stereo & Shar
leaning over & whispering
my secret:
"You'll always be a square at heart."

Waking Up Sober

the rain
        stopped dead

blue patches of sky
far off
        downriver.

Clumps of fog, wet

mist-swirl

in low gullies.

A steady hiss

    earth   sponge
        sucking water
           up.

A single bird call,
cow moo.

      Drying out.

The Roan Horse

The roan horse
by the red barn
standing, asleep

one hoof bent
      just touching
the ground

Book of Naming

milk glass

wrapped night-eye to cannon bone, pan candles
suppurating   (dust)
Nootka
Black outlined oat flake, purple scales
awns
Mullein
raceme
involucre's
anthers,   egrets

rhophalium

List of Essentials

Ransack garage. Sleeping bag, flashlight, tent
Stove, rain gear, maps, grill from barbeque.
Tarp. Saw. Kindling thrown into cardboard box.
Cook kit, silverware, propane. Warm clothes,
waders, boots, fly rod & flies. Book about
John Muir, wearing only a huge overcoat with bread
stuffed in pockets in the dead of winter. Yosemite.

Drought

October & the dry earth
like an oven
      trees standing
baked brown

Dying.

Down along the ground
      a breeze sneaks along
twisting under edge
of tent flap,
      licks across our faces

The river low
Crawling across burning rocks.

In the morning
      clouds like dolphins
      swimming away
Through clear steel blue flame air
Stillness at noon.

Grasshoppers go off like rockets
      from the tall dry grass

Wait for a change
      in the weather
For rain, for the wind
      to turn another page

Of the open unread book
lying on the sleeping bag

Separated from You

I go out of my run-down trailer
And walk along the river.
In the late afternoon
A dark brown otter
Scurries along the rocks.

He stops and looks at me.
When I move,
He darts
Under a rock.
I search, poking with sticks
To find him. Ten years—
Our life gone down some crevice
Like this.

A black vulture wheels
From the slope,
Flaps over my head,
Dips across the river,
Disappears into the black forest.

Back Home

(for James Wright)

Across the campground
Flames are high on the grill.
The steaks are sizzling.
The notes of a banjo
waft across to me.

My campfire is almost ashes.
And a beer. I have not yet
wasted my life.

Easter Sunday Alone

The hawk circles
Once, twice, as though
He's thinking
About going for my head.
Solitary, a figure
In a landscape, I jog along
The empty road
Far up the river,
The only moving target
In sight.

Beyond

My Mind Is a Closet

My mind is a closet
a dwarf lives in.
He doesn't sing or dance
but keeps his dim chest of
drawers filled with memories.
A hidden photo album waiting
to be dragged out again & again
flipped open by some chance
reverberation of thought dripping
in his brain & sends his tiny heart
scurrying like a hand touching
the glass knobs & stretching
pale fingers to feel, like insects,
into dark corners beneath
socks & underwear to touch
the forbidden photos, bring them
to light. Unposed snapshots,
simple names & dates scrawled
on back. He deals them out &
I see again the pictures called
"The Innermost Self" "The Real
Jim Thurber" & everyone's favorite:
"My Shame." I remember my blood
burned white-hot like a welder's torch.
Down the years I saw their images
every day until my heart
went slow enough to hold them
to the light again. Time and memory
conspire to keep me hunched
in this garret of mind where
only my dwarf lives, awaits
a timeless breeze of
uninvited silence, blows through
the darkness falls down
the curved & nameless
wind releases my breath
exhales it out over the light

floats on the wind grazing
rooftops & rising above
black trees out over
green valleys & beyond
up into flowing clouds
over mountains
above the town.

Jim Thurber's 115th Dream

I try to mop up the ocean
        from the pier
but my pail sinks
        out of sight
            through the green floor

The foreman walks back & forth
        on the water
spying on my futility.

At last a green rose rises
        in place of the sun at dawn
& places a thorn in my ear

(an alarm clock clicking like a camera shutter)

The disgusted foreman slings the mop downstairs
                & walks off the end of the pier

On My Forty-Third Birthday I Look Out
My Attic Window in a Small Town in Oregon

At dawn the oak tree limb outside the window
creaks with age, thumps softly against the house.
The soft lead-pencil sky draws lines of light
across the wall. Dreaming from the long night:
I'm in a tower looking down on a village.
It's France, an old war is going on, it's just
before the bombardment. The field of battle
is ringed by by gleaming hills of color.
Like a painting by Cézanne the scene falls apart
coalesces to a flat canvas of blocks & patches
of colors pressing against my eyes. The hours
stream away in wind, eye & sun topped roofs.
I start awake as the light opens a wound across
the grocery store's tin roof. Trucks & cars
start up & drive back & forth across the shaved body
of Main St. My head nods again while I think
who will remember their past? Who remembers
his birth? Who will remember coming to the end
ahead, his own death, & think that there
was any power?

Writing the Novel You Told Everyone About

It's only in the morning
when the fashionably dressed dreams
with their long fingers reluctantly
draw themselves back from touching
the blond damp curls on your pale neck
that I swear I will begin again
to love everyone & everything & stop
thinking & not go out & get involved again!
in some senseless activity connected
to saving the planet, especially the ring-tailed
green amphipod sloth in somebody's back yard

in Florida but to fucking stay here
with the tea on & some toast & the rain
beginning again & our white dog
with a black face standing heroic,
barrel chested in the back yard
beginning to drip enough to stink, wet,
banned from the house for now which
is fortuitous because of the 4,000 pages
left to write on the novel or 4,000 years—
whichever comes first but lately I've been
entering all the contests in the mail
to win enough to pay the bills threatening
to overflow & flood the floor, little white
malicious envelopes sailing toward pirate
infested waters of collector's attacks but
so what the bloodsuckers drained me
long ago, cut my juice, killed the phone,
plugged the water, nailed their liens
to the front door, notices of eviction
again fuck you, I'm writing a novel!
But first there's the letters to friends
& politicians & environmental causes
of the last minute last ditch blaring sirens
pleas for moola but I've drunk so much tea
getting ready to begin that I've got to piss—
for the third time & the rain so bad
I have to get up & let the dog in &
I'm starting to get very hungry
definitely no thoughts of any magnitude
today mebbe reread Kerouac to figure out
how he did it then get everything laid out
pencils sharpened, fresh page in the typewriter
if that doesn't work plan B will be to revise
an old poem and it will turn into
something completely different

that will take further revision tomorrow
but now it's time to mail the letters
which means getting into the car
& drive down to the post office
but it's already starting to get dark
so I better stay here & work on the novel
before you pull up in the driveway
coming home from work with my assurance
about the return of the dreams which
I think of right now as ghosts waiting
for me that make everything matter more
when I'm awake hoping to write a novel
everyone is sick of hearing about but
have to keep asking "How's the book going—
Sally & I can't wait to read it" & I think
about getting fake I.D. & disappearing
to Mexico or the tundra & wait for you
there in my new job as a free-lance
insurance salesman, professional house sitter,
stay at home house husband or as the deaf
guy unable to answer all the persistent questions
people ask you when you've been stupid
enough to tell them oh, I'm writing a novel

Looking Back

We believed we were going to change the world
We were angels of light unknowing
We were like the true children of Jesus
We fragged the nuclear family—left home
Flamed out of the Oedipal pressure cooker
We woke up America & put the fear into
The hearts of the authorities
And then sat there holding her hand
While she fell back to sleep again.
We embraced the infirm, the hopeless and the lost

We believed that we were all One
And the yellow, the brown, the black & the white
Were equal and we should hold hands lock arms
In a new solidarity of love
We believed that women should be released
From the prison they were put in, that their
Yoke should finally be lifted
We believed in our human sexual bodies
Freed from fear and suppression and oppression
We believed the power of love was greater
Than the power of war
We believed in the freedom to explore our consciousness
In every way in the search for knowledge and truth
We took a solemn vow to explore every avenue
Of our search for the divine fearlessly
We resisted the pigs, the fuzz, the blue meanies
The "get in the car" order signifying their fear
We kept asking the question "Why are innocent
People getting killed—by the millions?"
We infiltrated and corrupted the sanctimonious
Baptists and Catholics, Allah and Jaweh
We had no doubt that all our visions of Truth
Could ever be vanquished.
We were the ultimate cannon fodder.

When All Else Fails You

Fall against what's left:
the stillness there at the center of dawn,
mist rises like thin smoke off the river.
The first flash of silver—
fish rolling along the black currents.

Just after the sun raises its head,
like a stealthy Indian hunter
squinting over the rock cliff,
the fish sink deep again, wary
of that tiny slit of light. Now
the river reflects itself, the rocks
on the bottom disappear, the deep holes
are dark, impenetrable. Fear overcomes hunger.
Their wild abandon set aside,
the fish wait out the light.

Then, at dusk, the light escapes
the same way it appeared—in a time between two dots
on a stop watch that can't be measured.
An osprey launches
into a slow wheel overhead, her sharp
eyes looking for a telltale movement
breaking the river's surface.

The line yanks in my hand
hard, a last hungry trout
ripping the water, just before dark.

Sermon

       Don't turn away
from your only possibility
the times your body can touch
the times you gaze thru half-lidded eyes into the pleasure of hers
& the sounds you make together in the dark touching
her everywhere she's touching you
your guilt & shame cut loose this time forever
       gasps & thrills
              Eros rising
the love you wanted til it tore your dreams apart
      unlokd
         this grace
          of Beauty
(flicker like this candle in the dark) ?

The Green Book

There Is a Five-Fingered Sky

There is a five-fingered sky
& a woman growling in the next room

She fell off the waves & reappears as clouds
on the carbon copy

while the traffic separated by identities
endlessly goes in opposite directions

& toes are flutes wiggling
to escape shoes of mirrors

& breathing is only a rock
splitting the current

& Utrillo's telephone directory
dares the light

& hot beard beneath skin
& trees of tomorrow

& empty soldiers like bottles
w/out notes—flung away!

11/8/77

Their Work

The ardent dead know the earth
in ways we don't.
From underground
they toil to rest, yet
remain undisturbed.
Below it all,
so to speak.

The Story Teller

The wind is telling us a story.
The wind is always telling stories,
long, low and drawn out,
persistent until somehow
it gets in, underneath somewhere,
the door, around the window, it brings
its cutting edge inside
exhaling a cold breath
of icy syllables.

Sometimes the story
is so convoluted
it's a pain
in the ass like the wind
itself which might not stop.

Forever could happen
in the story or the other thing,
a strange calm like when
the wind stops, the story ends
and we sit there
musing in the silence.

Winter Storm

at dawn my eyes snap open like a shade rolling up
a blasting tympani of raindrops like metal bolts
screech out of the sky and slam down —
sheets of exploded water spark off roofs, car tops
ricochet crazily down the streets
fine needles of icy shrapnel expire
into thin liquid sheets running across the asphalt

down the gutters, down the pipes
down the storm drains through the sewers
out with the tides rivers streams creeks

out to the ocean out to the sea
home to the gray-black face
of the Tribesman Sky who waits,
his eyes closed his face hardened and blank
he chants with the wind whoops war
for the rain all night long

Eraser

Take the ordinary sky
out first,
the bluish-grey one with sun barely showing.
Next, rub off the view out the window

beginning with the forest across the river,
then the deck outside and then softly scrape away
the raindrops on the window and then
the window itself disappears. All that's left
are my feet laying across the end of the bed.

We could stop there like a breath drawn in and held.
Everything could be erased and then put back again
but it wouldn't be the same. It would be an approximation.
Everything can be wound and unwound,
At least we know that. What comes after
Everything is erased is a question.
I always stop at the border of all things.

Advice to Writers

She said how much she wished I wasn't broke
all the time so I talked to Allen Ginsberg
who supposedly wept in marketing research for years
loaded Greyhound buses worked menial tasks
and he told me with a straight face "to get a job."

The Mirror after 50

I've had to get bigger pants.
My hair is graying. The dentist said
my teeth looked like a 60 year old Eskimo's,
ground flat from grinding them 24/7.
Who knew you could get flattened tooth stubs
after a decade of stimulated living? I'd consider
this just the last of middle age but looking
in the mirror makes me long for
the peace of golden streets lauded in
church hymns while sitting there with the truly
elderly waiting for the Peace because they
might be right. Will it be peace, quiet, nothing, Nirvana?
Before I was manic depressive
I was manic depressive always split
between wanting to hurry it along
with something nonviolent — effective
but lethal and on the other hand, being
scared shitless of where I might
be going. The second glass of wine
soothes me. Maybe I'll live forever.

Heresies

Spiders

Spiders on ceiling can't write with spiders over my head
Thought spiders pull up covers keep me in bed til 3 pm
hurry out to street in pajamas I'm running down black street
I'm running in winter sun going down gold
running past black trees leafless arms pointed all directions
like snakes
I run out of the city open fields grass weeds cold sky cloudless
winter dusk
I'm running for the mountains far off I'm running away from
big hairy
red white blue spiders If I rest they're back scuttling inside
my brain
squeaking President bloated war budget 50% for shameful
dirty wars everywhere
locks up 2.3 million citizens at home more than all the rest of
the planet combined
More than China! More than Russia! Locks up black men
30% between 18-35 No escape for   fearful me they
take the wheel when I'm out driving
drive my brain past green hills up and around past wild river
farmhouse oak trees grow thick on hills fields full of lamb
ewes newborns
little tails twirling shorn they're naked February sun hills all
green pastoral
drive brain dead spiders shoot toxin in why can't I stop
THINKING?
Homeless starving tortured maimed wounded millions of
deaths fighting in
El Salvador Honduras Nicaragua killing in Colombia blast
Chile steal Peru
drop bombs experiment white phosphor skin burnt off Iraq
shoot remote drone missiles   Afghanistan beat gas
shoot Arabs whoops those rubber bullets live ammo Gaza West
Bank   Yemen Somalia whose killed where by whom U.S.?
Won't tell newspaper T.V. propaganda with   stenographic
conspiracy cover up FOIA redaction's leave totally blacked out pages

absolutely everything a state secret never before euphemisms
dreamed up "indefinite detention" "enhanced interrogation"
Arrest all turban wrapped boys girls wearing scarfs
charged with "material support" through
FBI entrapment terrorists in their mosques Bagram   new black
hole prison scratch A bu-Ghraib got new Guantanamo 700 US
bases in Afghanistan!
brain spiders dangle from brain like sucking leeches psst psst
what fumigator can kill them?
They'll rot in basement fuck up my mind Phew their sludge
pus cover the planet like
Sherwin Williams bloody paint ferment Capitalist Corporate
Multinational bankster Frankenstein SHIT!
Maybe shoveled by citizen brothers sisters on New Earth fields feed
homeless oppressed bankruptd foreclosure refugees demand free
health care end murder   sabotage war pipeline. Calling all
spiders! Calling all spiders! Surrender come in sign
organ   donor papers die now save the planet O save us Get out of
my head! Get out of my bed!   Dissolve disappear fuck off good
riddance don't need pills electroshock no suicide
Redwhite&blue spiders go extinct borders crumble nations dissolve
leave big circle shiny eyes   laugh laugh maybe love come down
& hold us in sweet arms breathe life kisses in all our bodies
waiting for Light!

Messages

Storms break in the mountains
thunder explodes over head
thudding into our sleep
War always fixed in our dreams.

House shudders
lightning snaps
snakes behind
our closed eyes.
Whole lakes of water
slopped on the town

two months late
tongues of dry ground
& empty rivers lapping
in panic of thirst

this watch
        on the spirit
                growth of man's vision
        nearing an end

America, this so-called nation & group of connected
natural continents around our sphere bent under
arrogant charade of benevolence papering over
greed, suspicion, hatred, unnatural division and now endless war

Actual human beings forced into overflowing World Jails
my mother my father my brother my son my daughter my sister
Indivisible these nations borders flags governments armies police

American jails lead the world   2.3 million prisoners—
30% black men & women

"A world where no thing thrives short of
        the total pestilence of its spirit" the poet declares

while the heart of silence is a harp
while the invisible hopes melt like pearls of snow
while the plucked strings break and love dies

The dispossessed know the daily miracle
        of survival
they rub it for luck like a rabbit's foot
they knock on wood cross themselves
make resolve to saints & ghosts
for one more day

—I know no history but this—

★

Eyes
overflowing w/ light
the voices speaking
the word
The Word which was
in the beginning
The Word which is Love

★

Rain swells tiny dry streams to torrents
Grizzly creek, Union creek, the North Fork and the South Fork
veins of the big river   dry trickles
of summer seepage   day drippers

boldly rolling now
boiling over
first rains of winter
February's aphrodisiac
of freshwater natal beckoning
to the salmon & steelhead
waiting to come home
offshore from the river
The wind arousing
the ocean to madness
in the distance

2000-2016

The Talking Point That Won't Die

No you can't have a pill
I won't water you today.
Heave your sleep & lay down.
Good dog, good dog
& don't cling to my ankles
sliding down & leaving burrs
plinking my skis.
Time out, look for
the fizzy goddam it.
If you can't sleep
get out. Leave me
holding the air.
I can't stop doing it
but you can.
O.K. Stay, wipe your
feet on the mat
as you go into shock—
the starry eye socket
of night's blow back,
you moan or say hello.

Sitting Mind

Where's Buddha when you need him?
Doesn't he work on weekends
to calm us down?

Where was he last night on TV —
60 seconds to go before some guy
with the swarthy skin & filthy beard,
who was also a blind deaf mute,
who might know the whereabouts
of the other guy with the suitcase bomb
ready to blow us all up?
And when torture didn't work they
decided to call Buddha in, could He
be reached in time? Where was He?

OK, sometimes he shows up
as Oscar Peterson & if you need
a poet to interpret, get Philip Whalen,
he's the best and cheap!

Buddha's usually out when I need Him.
But it's almost a sure bet to go for a walk,
dig the sky, sun, clouds, water, flowers —
snort the fresh scent of just mown grass,
duck the seagull shit, wheel
with the eagle, stalk like a heron,
watch out for rocks on the trail &

get yourself out of the way
of that rampaging red-eyed Elk herd
shaking the ground with thunder hooves,
charging across the meadow up ahead.

Buddha is cool, he's gonna show —
the further you walk, the more you breathe,
the less you think — poof
he steps out from behind a tree,
the most ordinary face
you'll ever see.

Going my way? he says,
flush with that mischievous grin.

Have You Found Your Lost Cause?

Have you found your lost cause?
I found my lost cause
before I lost my found cause
because cause & effect
birth and death
loving or hating
to nourish or to abandon
to kill or be killed
to destroy it to save it
to nuke the gay whales
to love it or leave it
to find all the body parts
to build some more jail cells
to bring home the homeless
to find the lost e-mails
to lose all the tear gas
flash grenades and taser guns

To your dead cause, Death!
to your cause
We live your effects
 Because this world is pain & suffering
because I love you no matter how much
I love you is not enough
to save us
to save the world
the world is its own lost cause
never to be found
looking down the rabbit hole
expanding is collapsing
the beginning is already the ending
of course the war is over
I'm starting another one today
        I can't stay in my skin
        tattooed with sin I found
        in my lost cause
        I have found my lost cause!

May 2008

A Night on the Town

Let's get loaded, she said
Let's get lost
tonight
in the warm rooms
of Castle Keep

These rooms
padded against the pain
we're
aloof,
high,
riding
on air
far out
on a sax note

Our bodies glistening
beneath the Pleasure
Dome, we'll be
the grateful,
numb
floating on emptiness
inside our rosy skulls.

Let's order room service
get greasy
with the baby
back ribs

Take my rib
and gnaw on it
Eat my bone & suck
my marrow out
while I lick
your skeleton
clean

& keep the jazz on
          we love jazz
jazz on the radio &
      make mine
              Miles

he's the Castle band
              The Kubla Khan quartet
Playing all night
              and on until noon
past our check out time
      while we're
              drinking Cold Duck
& eating toast & marmalade
              still lost & loaded

Was Every Stone a Purpose

Was every stone a purpose
first turned, the smooth white one
on a beach that marched
      ferociously inland without warning
      to open your veins to travel
      across countries, not just turning
      over stones instead wildly uprooting
      until there were only words left
      crack open like a pod
      filled with exotic seeds
      toxic though they were
      by then having traveled the world
      gambled away all of it
      received the transmission of the Dharma
      ended suffering and thus the World's
      suffering went back to the world
      of ordinary things to stand again
      on the beach aimlessly turning
      smooth wet stones satisfied
      You had found your lost cause.

Up Smith River Road

to George Daly

To thine own self be —
An autumn leaf
Crackling under foot

★

October. Golden leaves —
1,000 candles lit
in the green forest.
The dead can't see them.

★

I watch the black water,
The river moving with the tides.
A leaf falls from above — soundlessly.
Surprised,
I look up.

★

Through the trees,
The still pond.
Closer,
The ducks
wings flapping like gun shots,
Gone.

★

A breeze.
Yellow leaves drop
From branches.
Each one floating down
In its own way.
Some like parachutes
With tangled lines
Twirling straight down,

156

Some gliding back & forth
In long Z's like seabirds.
Others wobble and stall out
Like butterflies. Show offs
Snap from limbs,
Take a hard swan dive
Fall flat on the road—
Splat.

★

Spiders, I sweep
Away your cobwebs.
Don't you understand?

★

Silver nets by the hundreds
Advance in the grass.
Spiders, go home!

Book of Belongings

Daughter, You

Seed of my own
seed growing—

Your ear pressed
against seed table

of my heart you
are curled against

where no matter
is so important

that love can't
document its own

acceptances think
of ways

I am your father

true you are
my daughter

you were
born before

me, clouds
shape the

distant sounds
I know

time is without
peer—peers

everywhere is
omnidirectional

consciousness, O!

crawling on

your hands & knees
you chirp our

glad beginnings

Daughter at Four

Your hair is golden with fire.
The sun is gold with light in the fading afternoon.
The merry-go-round turns. Your eyes wide in
indecision: To be afraid or scream in delight.
On the patio around the ride an old couple polka
to the music. The sun goes down plunging a red-hot
poker through their clouding eyes. The heart of
the world is staked to the bottom of the cold ocean.

Daughter, will you ever know how love has cut
through my heart and takes you away?
Up and down and around you go.
Your mother plays Chopin until all the pianos
of the world turn and listen. Now you are four.
The calliope music throbs and bangs and tinkles.
You go by, innocent in the evening sunlight.
I will never forget you. You believe I will be
with you forever. Your chocolate stallion gallops
to a halt. My heart explodes like a thousand birds
of summer that turn into arrows of dying light,
fly through the empty rooms of my body
hurting the air. After the birds are gone it rains.
A heart drowns in a glass in an empty room.
A hand appears claiming to be love,
turns off the light and closes the door.

My House

I stand
under
the blue
skeleton
the sky
a structure
beyond
where I
am.

Wind & light
enter our space
filled with it
the act
of it
stopped.

This is
the house
that death
built this
is my
house

I live in
love I
understand.

Peace & Gladness

Poetry, be upon my lips as a star

Poetry, be upon my lips as a star
falling in the summer sky
& upon my breath as the breeze
springs up to cool the earth
each night. Oh Poems, be as
clear in your arrival as the love
you herald, by which this hand
starts up & writes & by which
my life is lived & would die of
wandering in search of
under clouds in these regions of
uncertainty, waiting for your
arrival to look through me
with your eyes of Truth.

Prayer

O happy clock in Space that ticks
To some vast Power
I pray to It
In night's last hour

Breath

The breath is an O
The breath is a ring joined at its narrowest spot
The breath disappears and reappears at that spot
where In becomes Out &
Out becomes In
The breath is behind everything
The breath moves but it isn't moving
The breath is the thing that doesn't move
when everything else
arises & disappears
The breath is there when you fall asleep
The breath is there when you wake up
The breath is still there when you travel to see

the Seven Wonders
of the world
The breath doesn't deal with illusions
When the breath stops at that tiniest point
or opens to a great flower
a Lotus
What does it find? What is it? Tell me only
You don't know you don't know

The breath is an O
a ring fused at the thinnest point
where In becomes Out and around again
Out becomes In

The breath is underneath it All

Court Filings

Why is the Sun filing a lawsuit
against The Weather Channel?
Filing states TWC deliberately
obscured the truth that the sun
is always shining somewhere
despite climate glaucoma
temporarily blurring the facts.
Can TWC prevail with co-defendants
like snowstorms, rain, smog, hurricanes catastrophic floods
solar eclipses, volcanic eruptions, tsunamis and earthquakes?
Friends of the Court, briefs filed by a host of speculative
John Does hope to also embed the possibility
of nuclear warfare or asteroid collisions

Even if the Sun should lose, TWC admits
that in the long run the Sun will win,
putting a snappy shoeshine on the planet
using a special polish dubbed
Hot Planet Wax.

Spring Dishes

Time to do the dishes!
Once a month?

1) clear out stacked up beer cans
like a munitions dump

2) strip to waist

3) drink 10 cups coffee

fill double steel sinks one
with soapy foam
other with hot rinse

4) attack glasses

tympani
glasses button & daisy
pink wine goblets
now
      one shattered
stem (dropped it)
Deep lake green scalloped tumblers
Minnesota pike waters
wide-mouthed sturdy
Never broke
a one of these

Delicate lavender smoke
convex impressionistic sides
More goblets!
Milk from goblets!
Wine from goblets!
Water from goblets!

Plain humdrum
clear glasses
short & tall

Ah discover under suds
Ruby traffic light red cut
glass tumblers
two sizes large
look like Santa Claus when
milk in them
Now some horny
stone ware filigreed
plates
bowls salad plates
egg shell white sloped
edges

5) Drain & reload
twin steel sinks fill
with hollow point special de-greasing
suds Bomb the sinks
with big sticky pots!

Drown crusted frying pans coffee pots
Beat them w/ stiff scrubbing brush!
Blast them w/ boiling faucet nozzle spray!
Mow down regiment of fetid silverware!
Acka acka acka acka acka!
Strafe knives forks spoons gravy
        ladles
soup spoons tea spoons spatulas pancake
turners egg beaters can opener apple peeler
wooden stir spoons metal tongs sieves cheese graters

6) Lay out big white bath towels across counters
heap hot rinsed kitchen amalgamation to dry—towel
    dry further if needed

7) Finish raking out garbage sweep
& mop floor polish counter tops wiped down
stove
Go outside pluck
single white rose from
bug-eaten leaves
pop in glass over sink
hello mama
the deed is done

Again

Love lights up my life like a flare
from thirty years ago. Close to you
your fragrance burns itself
across my body like radiation
that leaves a shadow of your essence,
a taste on my lips
and the corners of my mouth.
Who could wipe it away?

Destination

The archipelagos of your eyes are my destination.
I sail towards the islands of your Being.
Chart and compass, word & bone,
blood and faith, your Self shining
like a lighthouse across our endless nights.

Index to Poems

Afterword

I first met Jim Thurber in 2012 when my brother Desaix Anderson asked me to design *Mountains in Flight,* a book of Desaix's paintings and Jim's poems inspired by those paintings. What followed was an exhilarating exchange of ideas and tweaks. Jim was thoughtful, sweet, patient, and a wordsmith throughout — even his emails were poetic.

The chance to collaborate with Jim once again on *Zoo Chow* was a gift. His excitement over sorting through a lifetime of his writing for this book was infectious, his energy to keep writing new poems irrepressible, his calm and humor as he faced the inevitability of losing the battle against cancer inspiring.

Jim Thurber arrived in San Francisco in the early 1960s during the height of the San Francisco Renaissance and enrolled at San Francisco State. He described it as "a spontaneous gathering of poets from all over America who were writing a kind of new poetry — rebellious, wild, and original."

In 1964 he co-founded an underground magazine and wrote improvised poetry for passersby on the streets of North Beach. He noted that his mentors included "Desaix Anderson's gypsy band of southern intellectuals (in particular George Daly), California boogie mamas Lizaveta and the Goddess Diana, and gurus Chick Reeder and Silas Hoadley, along with many San Francisco poets — most notably Gary Snyder, Gregory Corso, and Ferlinghetti." Jim first read his poetry at the landmark Berkeley Poetry Conference in 1965.

Gail (Dusenbery) Chiarello recounts that she "met Jim Thurber in 1965 when we were two of the 'Nine Young Poets' who read on the last night of the Berkeley Poetry Conference. I had audited Gary Snyder's poetry seminar at UC Berkeley and studied with Robert Duncan at SF State. Jim and I shared a fascination with poetry, arguing, writing, publishing in the same little mimeographed magazines, along with Doug Palmer, Luis Garcia, Richard Denner, and the older San Francisco crowd of Michael McClure, Phil Whalen, Gary Snyder, Allen Ginsberg, and others. Allen Ginsberg took an enduring interest in Jim. For two years our lives centered around 'A Street' days, and we performed at poetry readings in Portland with Jaime Leopold's cabaret quintet, Padam Padam."

Jim returned to his beloved Pacific Northwest, with its "sweet rains, magnificent forests, rushing rivers and streams, waterfalls and mountains, and the vast Pacific Ocean of poetry." For his bio in *Mountains in Flight,* Jim described poetry as "an expressed reflection of the realization of the ineffable." In his own practice of poetry he believed "that the shortest distance between two points is unavailable to the poet, that the poet is just a passenger along for a ride in a vehicle that has no particular destination as it follows the unexpected twists and turns of words and language left to proceed by themselves."

For four decades, Jim lived in Oregon and continued his writing throughout his career as a postman. As Silas Hoagland tells the story, when Jim "finally emerged for us 40 years later, he was a retired rural postman who was able to care full-time for his family and deal with a liver cancer, and eager to see his poetry in print."

Chick Reeder, to whom Jim dedicated "Peyote the Kid," recalls:

"When we were in San Francisco as intense, if not frenetic, beginning students of Rev. Shunryu Suzuki, the Zen master, one Sunday evening Jim, along with Silas Hoadley, stepped through the kitchen window. Jim was in an aura of absolute innocence, ready to try everything! As we became close friends I began to realize that Jim was living a series of poems: from multidimensional incarnations of Puck the clown through a series of tragicomic love affairs to sitting zazen along with Snyder, Whalen, and us at the Oakland Army Terminal to protest Johnson's escalation of our presence in 'Nam. Manifesting every day the infinite spirit of exploration and invention, Jim rose like a spirit trout above the roiled currents of terrific creative and destructive energies—then he disappeared for forty years. It was like a miracle to find him again in southern Oregon! We took up where we had left off, but he had been living his poems all the while."

Doug Palmer and his wife, Jenny, visited the Thurbers in Oregon in 2016. "Jim battled health challenges, yet retained his fire, ability to laugh, and love of the written word. He and I took a walk with their little white dog, Foxy. Jim took the leash off Foxy, and Foxy took off in a rush, then stopping for us to catch up. That is what we wish we had for Jim. More time. Good moments as we come together. Jim's voice lives on in his writing, and his spirit lives on in our hearts. Rest in peace, my friend, Jim Thurber."

I am grateful to Gail, Doug, Silas, and Chick for adding their stories to this brief account, and I am forever grateful to be able to call Jim a friend. I miss answering the phone and hearing his soft, determined voice.

— Florence Anderson DeCell

A Note on the Art of Posthumous Editing

Authors typically accept responsibility for any and all errors in their books. At the outset of this remarkable *Zoo Chow* journey, Jim insisted that his spelling and formatting were not to be changed—except in the case of any errors he might make in re-typing his poems. Jim was unable to review the manuscript before he died; thankfully, Jim's longtime friend Jerry Butterfield stepped forward. To say that Jerry's encouragement, critical eye, and familiarity with Jim's voice were invaluable hardly describes his enormous contribution to the completion of this project. Jim's exuberant wordplay made it difficult at times to decide which version or what spelling; the actual title; was the unusual spacing always deliberate? Sometimes even a word: in "The Talking Point That Won't Die," Jim wrote: "No you can't have a pill / I won't water you today. / Heave your sleep & lay down." Heave? Have? We kept Heave, and hope that despite probable errors *Zoo Chow* honors Jim's creative vision.

www.ingramcontent.com/pod-product-compliance
Lightning Source LLC
Chambersburg PA
CBHW051726040426
42447CB00008B/991